THE CATHOLIC WRITER TODAY
AND OTHER ESSAYS

THE CATHOLIC
WRITER TODAY

AND OTHER ESSAYS

Dana Gioia

WISEBLOOD BOOKS • 2019

Cover art: George Tooker, *Embrace of Peace II*, 1988.
Egg tempera on gesso panel, 19 × 37 inches.
© Estate of George Tooker. Courtesy of DC Moore Gallery, New York.
Book designed and set in Calluna by Mark Askam,
and printed in the United States on acid-free paper.

Library of Congress Cataloging-in-Publication Data

Gioia, Dana, (1950-)
The Catholic Writer Today: and Other Essays / Dana Gioia;
1. Gioia, Dana 1950-
2. Poetry—History and Criticism
3. Christianity and Culture

ISBN 978-1-5051-1437-9, Paperback
ISBN 978-1-5051-1440-9, Hardcover

IN MEMORIAM

Sister Camilla Cecile
(1896-1985)
&
Sister Mary Damien
(1896-1982)

Who gave me piano and poetry

Gaudete in Domino semper

ACKNOWLEDGMENTS

These pieces first appeared, often in very different versions, in the following journals: *First Things, Hudson Review, Trinity Forum, Santa Clara Magazine, Crisis, Dappled Things, Presence, Christianity & Literature,* and *Image.* The two interviews were conducted as written exchanges with Robert Lance Snyder and Erika Koss. They are exercises in the classical form of the critical dialogue. The essay on St. Paul's Epistle to the Philippians was written for *Incarnation: Contemporary Writers on the New Testament,* edited by Alfred Corn. "To Witness Truth Uncompromised" was commissioned for *Martyrs: Contemporary Writers on Modern Lives of Faith,* edited by Susan Bergman. Father James Heft and the late Kevin Starr of the USC Institute for Advanced Catholic Studies helped clarify many of the ideas in these essays. The author wishes to thank the editors who accommodated his missed deadlines, compulsive revisions, and general disregard for assigned word count. God bless them, every one.

Contents

I

II

III

I

The Catholic Writer Today

I

*You shall know the truth, and
the truth shall make you odd.*
FLANNERY O'CONNOR

For years I've pondered a cultural and social paradox that diminishes the vitality and diversity of the American arts. This cultural conundrum also reveals the intellectual retreat and creative inertia of American religious life. Stated simply, the paradox is that, although Roman Catholicism constitutes the largest religious and cultural group in the United States, Catholicism currently enjoys almost no positive presence in the American fine arts—not in literature, music, sculpture, or painting. This situation not only represents a demographic paradox. It also marks a major historical change—an impoverishment, indeed even a disfigurement—for Catholicism, which has for two millennia played a hugely formative and inspirational role in the arts.

Roman Catholicism now ranks overwhelmingly as the largest religious denomination in the United States with more than 68 million members. (By contrast, the second largest group, Southern Baptists, has 16 million members.) Representing almost one quarter of the American population, Catholics also constitute the largest cultural minority in the nation. Supporting its historical claim of being the "universal" church, American Catholicism displays vast ethnic, national, linguistic, and social diversity. (In my first parish in Washington D.C., it was not unusual at Mass to see Congressional staffers, Central American immigrants, and urban homeless share the same pew.) While most Protestant churches continue to decline, Catholicism has grown steadily for the past two hundred years through a combination of immigration, births, and conversions. On purely demographic grounds, one would expect to see a huge and growing Catholic presence in the American fine arts.

If one asked an arts journalist to identify a major living painter or sculptor, playwright or choreographer, composer or poet, who was a practicing Catholic, the critic, I suspect, would be unable to offer a single name. He or she could surely identify a few ex-Catholics, such as Andres Serrano, Terrence McNally, or Mark Adamo, who use religious subject matter for satire, censure, or shock value. Catholic exposé is now a mainstream literary genre from the farcical (*Sister Mary Ignatius Explains It All*) to the tendentious (*The Gospel According to Mary Magdalene*). If the question were expanded to include novelists—the most sociological of major art forms—a well-informed literary critic might offer a few names such as Ron Hansen or Alice McDermott, authors whose subject matter is often overtly Catholic. Those few figures would account for most of the Catholic artists visible in our culture. The journalist's immediate reaction, however, would be to consider the question itself naïve or silly. Why would a serious critic even bother to know such cultish trivia? Nowadays the arts and Christianity seem only remotely connected, if at all. Contemporary culture is secular culture, is it not?

No one wants quotas for Catholic artists, but does it not seem newsworthy that the religion of one-quarter of the U.S. population has retreated to the point of invisibility in the fine arts? (Catholicism's position in popular entertainment is the subject for another essay.) There is a special irony that this disappearance has occurred during a period when celebrating cultural diversity has become an explicit goal across the American arts. Some kinds of diversity are evidently more equal than others. Has the decline generated cultural controversy? Not especially. Neither the arts world nor the Catholic establishment cares much about the issue. There seems to be a tacit agreement on both sides that, in practice, if not in theory, Catholicism and art no longer mix—a consensus that would have surprised not only Dante but also Jack Kerouac. The consequences of this situation are unfortunate—in different ways—for both the culture and the Church.

The issues at stake are large, complex, and surprisingly slippery. When the problem is discussed, which is seldom, even in Catholic circles, it typically invites abstraction, equivocation, threnody, and rant. To begin a responsible examination, it is necessary to define the topic carefully and then to stay factual and specific. Although the decline of Catholicism has occurred across the arts, this essay will focus on literature, which provides a useful perspective on all of the arts and their relation to the Church. Likewise, examining the situation of Catholic writers helps illuminate the current situation of all Christian writers.

II

From silly devotions, and sour-faced
saints, good Lord, deliver us.
ST. TERESA OF AVILA

Some definitions and distinctions—both religious and literary—are in order. To examine the situation of Catholic writers and literature, clarity will depend on defining those capacious categories. What is Catholic literature, and what makes an author a Catholic writer? I prefer to define both terms in strict and specific ways.

This essay concerns Catholic imaginative literature—fiction, poetry, drama, and memoir—not theological, scholarly, or devotional writing. Surprisingly little Catholic imaginative literature is explicitly religious; even less is devotional. Most of it touches on religious themes indirectly while addressing other subjects—not sacred topics but profane ones, such as love, war, family, violence, sex, mortality, money, and power. What makes the writing Catholic is that the treatment of these subjects is permeated with a particular worldview.

There is no singular and uniform Catholic worldview, but nevertheless it is possible to describe some general characteristics that encompass both the faithful and the renegade among the literati. Catholic writers tend to see humanity struggling in a fallen world. They combine a longing for grace and redemption with a deep sense of human imperfection and sin. Evil exists, but the physical world is not evil. Nature is sacramental, shimmering with signs of sacred things. Indeed, all reality is mysteriously charged with the invisible presence of God. Catholics also perceive suffering as redemptive, at least when borne in emulation of Christ's passion and death. Catholics also generally take the long view of things—looking back to the time of Christ and the Caesars while also gazing forward toward eternity. (The Latinity of the pre-Vatican II Church sustained a meaningful continuity with the ancient Roman world, reaching even into working-class Los Angeles of the 1960s where I was raised and educated.) Catholicism is also intrinsically communal, a notion that goes far beyond sitting at Mass with the local congregation, extending to a mystical sense of continuity between the living and the dead. Finally, there is a habit of spiritual self-scrutiny and moral examination of conscience—one source of *soi-disant* Catholic guilt.

The Catholic worldview does not require a sacred subject to express its sense of divine immanence. The greatest misunderstanding of Catholic literature is to classify it solely by its subject matter. Such literalism is not only reductive. It ignores precisely those spiritual elements that give the best writing its special value. The religious insights usually emerge naturally out of depictions of worldly existence rather than appear to have been imposed intellectually upon the work.

Catholic literature is rarely pious. In ways that sometimes trouble or puzzle both Protestant and secular readers, Catholic writing tends to be comic, rowdy, rude, and even violent. Catholics generally prefer to write about sinners rather than saints. (It is not only that sinners generally make more interesting protagonists. Their failings also more vividly demonstrate humanity's fallen state.) John Kennedy Toole's *A Confederacy of Dunces*, for example, presents a huge cast of characters, lost souls or reprobates all, who pursuing their assorted vices and delusions hilariously stumble toward grace and provisional redemption. The same dark comic vision pervades the novels of Evelyn Waugh, Anthony Burgess, and Muriel Spark. Ron Hansen's *Atticus* begins with the investigation of a murder. Flannery O'Connor's fiction is full of resentment, violence, and anger. "Good and evil appear to be joined in every culture at the spine," she observed, and violence is "strangely capable" of returning her characters "to reality and preparing them to accept their moments of grace." When Mary Karr titled her poetry collection *Sinners Welcome*, she could have been describing the Catholic literary tradition.

The question of who is or isn't a Catholic author also requires a few distinctions. The answer changes depending on how strictly or loosely one defines the term "Catholic." There are at least three degrees of literary Catholicism, each interesting in different ways. First, there are the writers who are practicing Catholics and remain active in the Church. Second, there are cultural Catholics, writers who were raised in the faith and often educated in Catholic schools. Cultural Catholics usually made no dramatic exit from the Church but instead gradually drifted away. Their worldview remains essentially Catholic, though their religious beliefs, if they still have any, are often unorthodox. Finally, there are anti-Catholic Catholics, writers who have broken with the Church but remain obsessed with its failings and injustices, both genuine and imaginary. All three of these groups have legitimate claims to literary attention. This essay, however, will focus mostly on the first group, with some references to the second. These individuals best qualify as Catholic writers, and yet they are currently the least visible in a literary culture where at present only the third group, the dissidents, has any salience.

III

There are in every man, at all times,
two simultaneous tendencies, one toward
God, the other toward Satan.

CHARLES BAUDELAIRE

One final and uncomfortable matter needs to be acknowledged and explained—the dubious moral character of many Catholic authors. Some great Catholic writers actually were saints—St. John of the Cross and St. Teresa of Avila. Thomas Aquinas proved a formidable poet when not writing theological tracts, as did the Blessed John Henry Newman. There are currently nascent efforts to canonize both G. K. Chesterton and Flannery O'Connor—two authors with a wicked sense of humor but exemplary moral character. (It may take more than the two customary miracles to get a great comic author officially enrolled in the Canon of Saints.) These were writers whose lives and works demonstrated heroic virtue. But not even every saint was always saintly. Remember the lusty young Augustine's devious prayer, "O, Lord, make me chaste, but not yet!"

Many Catholic writers have been conspicuously flawed individuals. When William Butler Yeats declared, "The intellect of man is forced to choose / Perfection of the life or of the work," he did not utter a universal truth, but his formula describes the careers of some major Catholic writers. Graham Greene's biography provides a catalogue of all seven deadly sins plus a few more of his own devising. Yet Greene remains a great Christian novelist. Muriel Spark was a horrifyingly cruel and negligent mother. She was nonetheless a comic writer of genius. The vagabond thief François Villon probably wrote his magnificent religious ballades while awaiting the gallows. (As Samuel Johnson remarked, "When a man knows he is to be hanged in a fortnight, it concentrates his mind wonderfully.")

Shouldn't Catholic writers lead lives in accordance with their faith? Of course, they should. And, alas, they don't always manage to.

Catholics are probably no better or worse behaved than any other denomination. Their main moral advantage nowadays is that they still recognize a sin when they commit one. "To be wicked is never excusable," wrote Charles Baudelaire, "but there is some merit in knowing that you are." That self-knowledge, however, does not necessarily translate into moral perfection, as Baudelaire's own doomed and dissipated life illustrated. In a fallen world, free will is hard to manage. At the very least, perhaps their faith made them less bad. When Nancy Mitford expressed her surprise that Evelyn Waugh could be so cruel and call himself a Christian, he replied, "You have no idea how much nastier I would be if I was not a Catholic. Without supernatural aid I would hardly be a human being." So, but for the grace of God, go us all.

In art, a flawed genius can produce a perfect masterpiece, even a religious one. *Parsifal*, *Lohengrin*, and *Tannhauser* are the three greatest Christian operas ever written (with the possible exception of Poulenc's *Dialogues of the Carmelites*). Both their magnificent words and music were created by Richard Wagner, a moral monster. I am relieved to report that Wagner wasn't Catholic, but the point remains that some artists can cultivate a pure and spiritual imagination amid a tainted life. I shall not explore this mystery in this essay, except to say that what concerns me here is not an author's moral character but the quality of his or her work and the authenticity of its Catholic vision.

If Catholic literature has a central theme, it is the difficult journey of the sinner toward redemption. Dante, no mean sinner himself, begins his *Commedia* with a confrontation of his own failings allegorized in three vicious animals—the lion, the she-wolf, and the leopard—symbolizing pride, lust, and violence. He then descends among the damned in hell to learn the true nature of evil. "This is what being a 'Catholic' poet really entails," wrote Elizabeth Jennings, "being willing to go to the edge of Hell itself in search of God and of Truth." Few make it back from the depths unscathed and immaculate. Perhaps it takes a sinner to convey the real meaning of damnation and redemption.

Even devout and joyful Catholic writers endure dark nights of the soul. Mystical insight exacts a price. Sanctity requires heroic virtue. Gerard Manley Hopkins, the master of ecstatic vision, wrestled with doubt and despair:

> No worst, there is none. Pitched past pitch of grief,
> More pangs will, schooled at forepangs, wilder wring.
> Comforter, where, where is your comforting?

Many Christian readers want inspiring books written by exemplary individuals who depict virtuous characters overcoming life's obstacles to arrive at happy endings. These readers should avoid most Catholic literature.

IV

An identity is not to be
found on the surface.
FLANNERY O'CONNOR

How can the current decline of Catholicism in American letters be accurately characterized? By what standard is it best measured and judged? One useful perspective is to go back to the middle of the previous century to analyze the two decades from the end of World War II in 1945 to the death of Flannery O'Connor in 1964. The comparison between the postwar era and today is illuminating, even shocking.

Sixty years ago Catholics played a prominent, prestigious, and irreplaceable part in American literary culture. Indeed, they played such a significant role that it would be impossible to discuss American letters in the mid-twentieth century responsibly without both examining a considerable number of observant Catholic authors and recognizing the impact of their religious conviction on their artistry.

These writers were prominent across the literary world. They included established fiction writers—Flannery O'Connor, Katherine Anne Porter, Walker Percy, J. F. Powers, Ernest Hemingway, Paul Horgan, Jack Kerouac, Julien Green, Pietro di Donato, Hisaye Yamamoto, Edwin O'Connor, Henry Morton Robinson, and Caroline Gordon. (Sociologist Father Andrew Greeley had yet to try his formidable hand at fiction.) There were also science fiction and detective writers such as Anthony Boucher, Donald Westlake, August Delerth, and Walter Miller, Jr. whose *Canticle for Leibowitz* remains a classic of both science fiction and Catholic literature.

There was an equally strong Catholic presence in American poetry, which included Allen Tate, Robert Lowell, Robert Fitzgerald, John Berryman, Kenneth Rexroth, Isabella Gardner, Phyllis McGinley, Claude McKay, Dunstan Thompson, John Frederick Nims, Brother Antoninus (William Everson), Thomas Merton, Josephine Jacobsen, and the Berrigan brothers, Ted and Daniel. These writers represented nearly every aesthetic in American poetry. There were even Catholic haiku poets, notably Raymond Roseliep and Nick Virgilio.

Meanwhile the U.S. enjoyed the presence of a distinguished group of Catholic immigrants, including Jacques Maritain, Czeslaw Milosz, Dietrich von Hildenbrand, Henri Nouwen, René Girard, John Lukacs, Padraic and Mary Colum, José Garcia Villa, Alfred Döblin, Sigrid Undset, and Marshall McLuhan. Some of the writers came to the U.S. to flee Communism or Nazism. (Jesuit philosopher Pierre Teilhard de Chardin came here, late in life, to flee the European Catholic hierarchy.) These writers were supported by engaged Catholic critics and editors with major mainstream reputations, such as Walter Kerr, Wallace Fowlie, Hugh Kenner, Clare Boothe Luce, Robert Giroux, William K. Wimsatt, Thurston Davis, and Walter Ong. The intellectual milieu was further deepened by "cultural Catholics" whose intellectual and imaginative framework had been shaped by their religious training—writers such as Eugene O'Neill, John O'Hara, J. V. Cunningham, James T. Farrell, John Fante, Mary McCarthy, and John Ciardi, as well as—at the end of this period— John Kennedy Toole, Andre Dubus, and Belfast-born Brian Moore.

The cultural prominence of mid-century American Catholic letters was amplified by international literary trends. The British "Catholic Revival" led by writers such as Graham Greene, Evelyn Waugh, J.R.R. Tolkien, Edith Sitwell, Ronald Knox, Hilaire Belloc, David Jones, Muriel Spark, Elizabeth Jennings, and Anthony Burgess provided a contemporary example of how quickly a Protestant and secular literary culture could be enlivened by new voices. (G.K. Chesterton had died in 1936, but he continued to exercise enormous influence on both British and American writers.) At the same time in France another Catholic revival had emerged guided by novelists Georges Bernanos and François Mauriac and poets Paul Claudel and Pierre Reverdy, all of whom were widely read in the U.S. Another factor inspiring American Catholic authors, a disproportionate number of whom were Irish-American, was the rise of modern Irish literature. Long the province of Protestants, twentieth-century Irish letters suddenly spoke in the Catholic accents of writers such as James Joyce, Sean O'Casey, Frank O'Connor, and Flann O'Brien. Not surprisingly, American Catholic writers of this period saw themselves as part of an international movement.

V

The crowded stars seemed bent
upon being understood.
G. K. CHESTERTON

The explosion of American Catholic writing in the two decades after World War II has sometimes been described as a renaissance or revival, but these attractive terms are misnomers. There was no earlier American Catholic literary tradition to be reborn. Until the war years, American literature had been mostly a Protestant affair seasoned by a scattering of Jewish voices (with both groups becoming increasingly secular). Although Catholics had ranked as the nation's largest religious denomination since 1890, there were social, linguistic, educational, and cultural barriers that slowed their literary development. Despite the success of a few popular figures, such as Joyce Kilmer, there had been almost no literature of enduring significance. It took half a century of growth and progress in Catholic schools and universities, journalism and publishing to make the mid-twentieth-century achievement possible. The period from 1945 to 1964 represented the first full flowering of the American Catholic imagination—a powerful expansion of the national literature, which impressed both the pagan and the pious with its energy, depth, and originality. It was not a rebirth but a nativity—the sensibility of an ancient faith heard in a new world for the first time. The poor, immigrant communities that had reshaped the American population now helped reconfigure American letters.

The postwar decade was not a period of Catholic literary dominance, which is not, to my mind, an attractive or desirable goal. It was, instead, an era in which Catholic voices in all their diversity played an active role in shaping the dynamic public conversation that is American literature. Catholicism was not only seen as a worldview consistent with a literary or artistic vocation; rich in rituals, signs, and symbols, the Roman church was often regarded as the faith most compatible with the artistic temperament. It was never surprising to hear that some writer had converted, be it the young Robert Lowell or Ernest Hemingway, the middle-aged Allen Tate or Edith Sitwell, the older Tennessee Williams or Claude McKay, or even the dying Wallace Stevens or Jaime de Angulo. After all, as another deathbed convert, Oscar Wilde, remarked, "Catholicism is the only religion to die in."

Sixty years ago it was taken for granted that a significant portion of American writers were Catholics who balanced their dual identities as artists and believers. These writers published in the mainstream journals and presses of the time as well as with specifically Catholic journals and presses. They also won major literary awards. Between 1945 and 1965 Catholic novelists and poets received 11 Pulitzer Prizes and 5 National Book Awards (6 NBAs if one counts O'Connor's posthumously published *Complete Stories* in 1972).

Catholic authors were reviewed and discussed in the general press. They were also intelligently covered in the large and varied Catholic press. Thomas Merton, for example, published with Harcourt Brace, New Directions, and Farrar Straus and Cudahy, as well as small monastic and ecclesiastical presses. He was reviewed in *Time*, *Life*, *Atlantic Monthly*, and *Saturday Review* as well as *Commonweal*, *Ave Maria*, *Catholic World*, and *Theology Digest*. Writers also had the opportunity, if they were so inclined, to reach a Catholic audience directly in person on a large speakers' circuit of religious schools and associations. Although crippled by lupus, Flannery O'Connor helped pay the family bills on the lecture circuit. She visited colleges, conferences, seminaries, and even a convent of cloistered nuns. She found travel tiring, but she often enjoyed the people she encountered. "When you assume that your audience holds the same beliefs as you do," she declared, "you can relax a little."

It is instructive to see how large and substantial the Catholic literary subculture once was and how much it influenced literary coverage in the general press. Reading through Flannery O'Connor's published interviews, a scholar today might be surprised to see that half of them appeared in Catholic journals—an inconceivable situation now for a serious young writer. Equally inconceivable, the secular journals asked her informed and respectful questions about the relation of her faith to her art. The mid-century Catholic writer could address both the general reader and the Catholic reader—knowing that both audiences were not only on speaking terms but also overlapped.

VI

Looking back on the mid-century era of O'Connor, Merton, Porter, and Tate, one could summarize the position of American Catholic literary culture with four characteristics. First, many important writers publicly identified themselves as faithful Catholics. Second, the cultural establishment accepted Catholicism as a possible and permissible artistic identity. Third, there was a dynamic and vital Catholic literary and intellectual tradition visibly at work in the culture. Fourth and finally, there was a critical and academic milieu that actively read, discussed, and supported the best Catholic writing. Today not one of those four observations remains true. Paradoxically, despite the social, political, economic and educational advancement made by Catholics over the past half century, our place in literary culture has dramatically declined. In order to describe the current situation, we would have to restate each of the observations in a radically different form.

Sixty years ago many established writers identified themselves as faithful Catholics. Today there are still a few writers who admit to being practicing Catholics, such as Ron Hansen, Alice McDermott, Mary Karr, Tobias Wolff, or Richard Rodriguez, but they seem notable exceptions in an aggressively secular literary culture. Many Catholic authors follow their faith quietly. More significant, most young writers no longer see their religion as a core identity—in spiritual or aesthetic terms. Their faith is something to be hidden or discarded in order to achieve success in an arts world that appears hostile to Christianity. In practical terms, who can blame them?

Sixty years ago there were many famous literary conversions to Catholicism. These haven't stopped altogether. Not long ago there were the celebrated literary "bad girl" and "bad boy" conversions of

Mary Karr and Franz Wright. (There is more rejoicing in heaven over one lost poet found than in 99 novelists who have never strayed.) Now, however, the most common form of "conversion" is among artists who leave the Church. Some writers have made leaving the faith a recurring habit. Vampire novelist Anne Rice has publicly rejoined and renounced the Church twice.

The second observation that the cultural establishment once accepted Catholicism as a possible and permissible artistic identity, also needs to be substantially revised. Today the cultural establishment views faithful Catholics with suspicion, disdain, or condescension. From its earliest stages, American society has displayed a streak of anti-Catholicism, which originated in Protestant, especially Puritan, antagonism toward Rome. Anti-Papist hatred became an enduring element in populist bigotry as exemplified by the Know-Nothings and Ku Klux Klan. This ingrained bias was perpetuated by class prejudice against the waves of poor immigrants—first the Irish, Italian, German, Polish, Hungarian, Mexican, and later the Filipino, Cuban, Puerto Rican, Vietnamese, Haitian, and Central American poor who came to the U.S. in search of a better life. The American Catholic Church has historically been the church of immigrants and the poor. Consequently, the Roman faith has often been viewed as one of the backward beliefs these dispossessed groups brought over from the Old Country.

Anti-Catholicism has also been common among the intelligentsia. As Patrick Moynihan observed, anti-Catholicism remains "the one respectable form of intellectual bigotry." During the ceremony when O'Connor was posthumously awarded the National Book Award, her editor Robert Giroux recalled one literary celebrity complaining, "Do you really think Flannery O'Connor was a great author? She's such a Roman Catholic." Would anyone have made a similar remark at the ceremonies honoring Philip Roth or Ralph Ellison? As poet-historian Peter Viereck commented, "Catholic baiting is the anti-Semitism of liberals." But the Left enjoys no monopoly on anti-Catholicism. Despite some ecumenical progress in recent years, it remains a persistent prejudice among Southern fundamentalists and evangelicals. A New York leftist and an Alabama Pentecostal may not agree on much, but too often they share a dislike of Catholics.

Despite a public culture committed to diversity and tolerance, anti-Catholicism has grown measurably worse among academics and intellectuals over the past decade—driven in equal parts by sexual abuse scandals, gay rights, resurgent atheism, and lingering historical prejudice. At best, Catholicism is seen as a private concern rather than a public identity and certainly not an advisable or reliable basis for a personal aesthetic. As the British novelist Hilary Mantel recently declared, "Nowadays the Catholic Church is not an institution for respectable people."

The third observation that there was a dynamic and vital Catholic literary tradition also needs to be revised. There is currently no vital or influential Catholic tradition evident in mainstream American culture. The few distinguished writers who confess their Catholicism appear to work mostly in isolation. Such isolation may not hamper their creativity. Hansen, McDermott, Rodriguez, and Wolff rank among the nation's finest authors. But their lack of a collective public identity limits their influence—as Catholics—both on the general culture and young writers. Meanwhile the less-established writers, who have made Catholicism the core of their artistic identity, work mostly outside mainstream literary life in a small Catholic sub-culture that has little impact on general cultural life.

Finally, the fourth observation that there was a critical and academic milieu that discussed and supported the best Catholic writing, perhaps needs to be revised the least, but the current situation reveals a substantially diminished scene. There has been a vast retrenchment of this intellectual milieu. (This trend has been aggravated by the many Catholic colleges and universities that now seem socially embarrassed by their religious identity.) There is still a small, imperiled, and largely segregated cohort of Catholic magazines such as *Commonweal*, *America*, and *Crisis*. There are also serious ecumenical publications such as *First Things* and *Image,* as well as scholarly ones such as *Christianity & Literature* and *Renascence*. Their collective reach and readership has declined, and they stand at a greater distance from mainstream culture than their equivalents did sixty years ago. The influence of these journals, even the largest like *First Things* and *Commonweal*, is limited to a shrinking subculture. Moreover, few Catholic journals still publish a substantial number of book reviews or provide much literary coverage. Consequently, they provide neither much employment for Catholic critics who seek to write for their own community nor significant exposure for emerging authors.

What is the effect of this intellectual segregation? The Catholic voice is heard less clearly and less often in the public conversations that inform American culture. Consequently, Catholics have lost the power to bring their own best writers to the attention of a broader audience. Today, if any living Catholic novelist or poet has a major reputation, that reputation has not been made by Catholic critics but by the secular literary world, often in spite of their religious identity. In literature at least, the Catholic media no longer command sufficient cultural power to nominate or effectively support what is best from their own community. Has this situation disturbed Catholic leaders? Not especially. The Catholic subculture seems conspicuously uninterested in the arts.

What absorbs the Catholic intellectual media is politics, conducted mostly in secular terms—a dreary battle of Right versus Left for the soul of the American Church. If the soul of Roman Catholicism is to be found in partisan politics, then it's probably time to shutter up the chapel. If the universal Church isn't capacious enough to contain a breadth of political opinion, then the faith has shriveled into something unrecognizably paltry. If Catholic Christianity does not offer a vision of existence that transcends the election cycle, if our redemption is social and our resurrection economic, then it's time to render everything up to Caesar.

Wallace Stevens remarked that "God and the imagination are one." It is folly to turn over either to a political party, even your own.

If American Catholicism has become mundane enough to be consumed by party politics, perhaps it's because the Church has lost its imagination and creativity.

VII

Many people judge a religion by its art,
and why indeed shouldn't they?

ELIZABETH JENNINGS

In the literary sphere, American Catholics now occupy a situation closer to that of 1900 than 1950. It is a cultural and religious identity that exists mostly in a marginalized subculture or else remains unarticulated and covert in a general culture inclined to mock or dismiss it. Among the "respectable people" Hilary Mantel mentioned, Catholicism is retrograde, déclassé, and disreputable. No wonder Catholic writers keep a low profile. After all, what do writers gain now by identifying themselves as Catholics? There is little support from within the community—not even the spiritual support of an active artistic tradition. The general intellectual and academic culture remains at least tacitly anti-Catholic. The situation brings to mind Teresa of Avila's witty complaint, "If this is the way You treat your friends, no wonder You have so few."

If one needs an image or metaphor to describe our current Catholic literary culture, I would say that it resembles the present state of the old immigrant urban neighborhoods our grandparents inhabited. They may still have a modicum of local color amid their crumbling infrastructure, but they are mostly places from which upwardly mobile people want to escape. Economically depressed, they offer few rewarding jobs. They no longer command much social or cultural power. To visualize the American Catholic arts today, don't imagine Florence or Rome. Think Newark, New Jersey.

A different person might summarize the situation slightly differently, or argue with the phrasing of particular observations, but I doubt that any honest observer of current literary culture could refute this sad summary of Catholic letters today. Despite its proclamations of diversity and multiculturalism, contemporary American letters has little use for Catholicism, and Catholics have retreated from mainstream cultural life.

By now I have surely said something to depress, anger, or offend every reader of this essay. It depresses me, too, but I won't apologize. If I have outlined the cultural situation of Catholic writers in mostly negative terms, it is not out of despair or cynicism. It is because to solve a problem, we must first look at it honestly and not minimize or deny the difficulties it presents. If we want to revitalize some aspect of cultural life, we must understand the assumptions and forces that govern it.

The collapse of Catholic literary life reflects a larger crisis of confidence in the Church that touches on all aspects of religious, cultural, and intellectual life. What I have said so far also pertains, in general terms, to all American Christians. Whatever their denomination, they have increasingly disengaged themselves from artistic culture. They have, in effect, ceded the arts to secular society. Needless to say, for Catholicism, this cultural retreat—indeed, this virtual surrender—represents a radical departure from the Church's traditional role as patron and mentor to the arts. In only fifty years the patron has become the pariah.

VIII

*It is the test of a good religion
whether you can joke about it.*

G. K. CHESTERTON

The schism between Christianity and the arts has had two profound consequences, two vast impoverishments—one for the arts world, the other for the Church. First, for the arts world, the loss of a transcendent religious vision, a refined and rigorous sense of the sacred, the breaking and discarding of two thousand years of Christian mythos, symbolism, and tradition has left contemporary American art spiritually diminished. The shallow novelty, the low-cost nihilism, and the vague and sentimental spiritual pretensions of so much contemporary art—in every media—is the legacy of this schism, as well as the cynicism that pervades the arts world.

This last point needs to be clarified to avoid any misunderstanding. Art does not need to be religious. There are great masterpieces that have no hint of religious transcendence. What I am suggesting is something more subtle and complex. Culture is a conversation. A vigorous culture contains different voices, often in active debate. The voice of religious faith enlarges and enlivens the overall dialectic of culture, even among non-believers, just as the voice of secular society keeps religious writers more alert and intelligent. Once you remove the religious as one of the possible modes of art, once you separate culture from the long-established traditions and disciplines of spirituality, you don't remove the spiritual hungers of either artists or audience. You satisfy them more crudely with the vague, the pretentious, and the sentimental. The collapse of the culture that supported O'Connor and Porter, Powers and Merton led to the culture that consumes teen paranormal romances, ghost reality shows, and internet wiccans.

The great and present danger to American literature is the growing homogeneity of our writers, especially the younger generation.

Often raised in several places in no specific cultural or religious community, educated with no deep connection to a particular region, history, or tradition, and now employed mostly in academia, the American writer is becoming as standardized as the American car—functional, streamlined, and increasingly interchangeable. The globalization so obvious in most areas of the economy, including popular culture, has had a devastating impact on literature. Its influence is especially powerful since globalized commercial entertainment—movies, television, popular music, and video games—now shapes the imagination of young writers more pervasively and continuously than do literary texts. An adolescence in Los Angeles is not much different from one in Boston or Chicago when so many thousands of hours are spent identically in the same virtual worlds. Is it any wonder that so much new writing lacks any tangible sense of place, identifiable accent, or living connection to the past? Nourished more by global electronic entertainment than active individual reading, even the language lacks resonance and personality. However stylish and efficient, writing with no past probably has no future.

If you dislike Christianity—which some readers of this essay surely do—you may regard the decline of Catholic literature as a sign of progress. It seems proof positive that contemporary Christianity lacks creativity and cultural intelligence. But even in secular terms, this position is myopic and self-defeating (not to mention undemocratic). The retreat of the nation's largest cultural minority from literary discourse does not make art healthier. Instead, it weakens the dialectic of cultural development. It makes American literature less diverse, less vital, and less representative.

There is a temptation for members of a cultural elite to see their values as the only respectable virtues, a tendency that blinds the group to both cultural innovation and aesthetic dissent, especially from people deemed marginal to established intellectual society. Jazz, blues, film, detective fiction, science fiction, and photography were all arts that emerged without elitist approval, and yet they all made indisputable contributions to American culture. In retrospect, it seems clear that the great accomplishments of mid-twentieth-century American fiction depended on the emergence of Jewish, Catholic, and African American voices. These distinctively accented voices—Saul Bellow and Bernard Malamud, Flannery O'Connor and J. F. Powers, Ralph Ellison and James Baldwin—opened up new vistas of American fiction by articulating the worldview of groups previously marginal. People on the margins see some things more clearly than do those privileged to live at the center. When the elite and the powerful silence the voices of outsiders, culture hardens into convention. Any secular reader who wishes Catholic voices away unknowingly furthers the narrowing and standardization of American letters.

The second consequence of this cultural schism affects the Church. The loss of the aesthetic sensibility in the Church has weakened its ability to make its call heard in the world. Dante and Hopkins, Mozart and Palestrina, Michelangelo and El Greco, Bramante and Gaudi have brought more souls to God than all the preachers of Texas. The loss of great music, painting, architecture, poetry, sculpture, fiction, and theater has limited the ways in which the Church speaks to people both within and beyond the faith.

Catholicism rightly revels in its theological and philosophical prowess, which is rooted in two millennia of practice and mastery. Theology is important, but formal analytical thought—the *splendeur et misère* of Roman Catholicism—is not the primary means by which most people experience, accept, or reject a religious faith. They experience the mysteries of faith (or fail to) in the fullness of their humanity—through their emotions, imagination, and senses as well as their intellect. Until recently, a great strength of Catholicism has been its glorious physicality, its ability to convey its truths as incarnate. The faith was not merely explained in its doctrine but reflected in sacred art, music, architecture, and the poetry of liturgy. Even St. Thomas Aquinas knew there were occasions to put theology aside and write poetry. His resplendent verses are still sung with incense at Eucharistic Benediction. "Bells and incense!" scoffs the Puritan, but God gave people ears and noses. Are those organs of perception too humble to bring into church? For very good reason, participating in Mass involves all five senses. We necessarily bring the whole of our hairy and heavy humanity to worship.

Nowhere is Catholicism's artistic decline more painfully evident than in its newer churches—the graceless architecture, the formulaic painting, the banal sculpture, the ill-conceived and poorly performed music, and the cliché-ridden and shallow homilies. Saddest of all, even the liturgy is as often pedestrian as seraphic. Vatican II's legitimate impulse to make the Church and its liturgy more modern and accessible was implemented mostly by clergy with no training in the arts. These eager, well-intentioned reformers not only lacked artistic judgment; they also lacked a respectful understanding of art itself, sacred or secular. They saw words, music, images, and architecture as functional entities whose role was mostly intellectual and rational. The problem is that art is not primarily conceptual or rational. Art is holistic and incarnate— simultaneously addressing the intellect, emotions, imagination, physical senses, and memory without dividing them. Two songs may make identical statements in conceptual terms, but one of them pierces your soul with its beauty while the other bores you into catalepsy. In art, good intentions matter not at all. Both the impact and the meaning of art are embodied in the execution. Beauty is either incarnate, or it remains an intangible abstraction.

Whenever the Church has abandoned the notion of beauty, it has lost precisely the power that it hoped to cultivate—its ability to reach souls in the modern world. Is it any wonder that so many artists and intellectuals have fled the Church? Current Catholic worship often ignores the essential connection between truth and beauty, body and soul, at the center of the Catholic worldview. The Church requires that we be faithful, but must we also be deaf, dumb, and blind? I deserve to suffer for my sins, but must so much of that punishment take place in church?

IX

In such a culture, in such a Church, in such a time, what is the
Catholic writer to do? Isolated, alienated, discredited, ignored, how
can he or she survive, let alone prosper? Aren't things too far gone
to change? The answer can only be . . . of course not. Times are
always bad. Culture is always in trouble. The barbarian is always at
the gate, and some part of the Church inevitably needs a good
sweeping. *O tempora! O mores!* is a perpetual complaint. As every
Catholic knows, we live in a fallen world where—*o felix culpa*—we
rejoice in the possibilities of redemption.

For the artist, every problem represents a sort of opportunity. The
necessary insight here is that history doesn't solve problems, culture
doesn't solve problems; only people do. The history of the Church
and the history of art repeatedly demonstrate that a few people of
sufficient passion, courage, and creativity can transform an age. If
we learn nothing else from the lives of the saints, we should know
the power their works and examples had to change an age. St. Francis
of Assisi had a greater impact on European society than any ruler of
the Holy Roman Empire.

New artistic movements originate in similar ways. They grow out
of the efforts of a few catalytic individuals who reject a bankrupt or
moribund status quo and articulate a compelling new vision. French
Symbolism and English Romanticism, both of which became transformative international movements, each began with a handful
of writers. Once the new vision is articulated and embodied in
masterful works, it spreads quickly, indeed indomitably—uniting
people in a common cause. The success of cultural and religious
movements inevitably reveal that many people already share the
new ideals but do not feel empowered until there is a credible public

call to action. The real challenge is not in the number of participants but in the arrival of a few powerful innovators who can serve as cultural catalysts. Two great poets are stronger than two thousand mediocrities.

The Catholic writer really needs only three things to succeed: faith, hope, and ingenuity. First, the writer must have faith in both the power of art and the power of the spirit. The cynicism that pervades contemporary cultural life must be replaced by a deep confidence in the human purposes and importance of art. Art is not an elitist luxury or a game for intellectual coteries. It is a necessary component of human development, both individually and communally. Art educates our emotions and imagination. It awakens, enlarges, and refines our humanity. Remove it, dilute it, or pervert it, and a community or a nation suffers—becoming less compassionate, curious, and alert, more coarse, narrow, and self-satisfied.

The Catholic writer must also recover confidence in his or her own spiritual, cultural, and personal identity. How can I, for example, as an Italian and Mexican American understand myself without acknowledging the essential link with Catholicism? It is in my cultural DNA—from generations of ancestors. Catholicism is my faith, my heritage, my worldview, my mythology, and my community. Banish or deny that spiritual core—for whatever reason—and I lose some of my authenticity as an artist. This loss is surely part of the agony so tangible in the writing of ex-Catholics. It hurts to renounce part of your own identity, even if you consider the abnegation a necessity. Who can blame them for writing with such passion about the Church? Even a phantom limb can cause excruciating pain. They rightly refuse to become homogenous and generic writers in a global secular culture. They no longer have a spiritual home, except in their dissent.

A Catholic writer must also have hope. Hope in the possibilities of art and one's own efforts. Hope in the Church's historical ability to change as change is needed. The main barrier to the revival of Catholic writing and the rapprochement of faith and the arts is despair, or perhaps more accurately *acedia*, a torpid indifference among precisely those people who could change the situation—Catholic artists and intellectuals. Hope is what motivates and sustains the writer's enterprise because success will come slowly, and there will be many setbacks.

Finally, there is a third element that has nothing to do with religion. The Muse is no Calvinist. She does not believe that faith alone justifies an artist. The writer needs good works—good literary ones. The goal of the serious Catholic writer is the same as that of all real writers—to create powerful, expressive, memorable works of art. As Flannery O'Connor observed, "The Catholic novelist doesn't have to be a saint; he doesn't even have to be a Catholic; he does, unfortunately, have to be a novelist." The road to Damascus may offer a pilgrim sudden and miraculous intervention, but faith provides no shortcuts on the road to Parnassus.

All writers must master the craft of literature, the possibilities of language, the examples of tradition, and then match that learning with the personal drive for perfection and innovation. There is a crippling naiveté among many religious writers (and even editors) that saintly intentions compensate for weak writing. Such misplaced faith (or charity) is folly. The Catholic writer must have the passion, talent, and ingenuity to master the craft in strictly secular terms while never forgetting the spiritual possibilities and responsibilities of art. That is a double challenge, but it does ultimately offer a genuine advantage. If faith provides no shortcuts to Parnassus, once the literary pilgrim attains the summit, it does afford him or her a clearer vision. The Catholic writer has the inestimable advantage of a profound and truthful worldview, that has been articulated, explored, and amplified by two thousand years of art and philosophy, a tradition whose symbols, stories, personalities, concepts, and correspondences add enormous resonance to any artist's work. To be a Catholic writer is to stand at the center of the Western tradition in artistic terms.

41

This perspective is invaluable in times, like ours, of intellectual confusion. The Catholic writer understands the necessary relationship between truth and beauty, which is not mere social convention or cultural accident but an essential form of human knowledge—intuitive, holistic, and experiential. Art is a form of knowing—distinct and legitimate—rooted in feeling and delight—that discovers, in the words of Jacques Maritain, "The splendor of the secrets of being radiating into intelligence." That insight makes possible the great potential of Christian literature to depict the material world, the physical world of the senses, while also revealing behind it another invisible and eternal dimension.

X

How long, I wondered, could this thing last?
But the age of miracles hadn't passed.
IRA GERSHWIN

The renewal of the Catholic arts will not come from the Church itself. I am prepared to believe in miracles, but the notion that the Catholic hierarchy will make literature and the arts a priority and then exercise good judgment in supporting them exceeds all credulity. The bishops may occasionally recite some high-minded cant on the subject of culture, but their passions lie elsewhere. They have more pressing problems to address, including some of their own making. Ecclesiastical indifference, however, is a great blessing—perhaps even the miracle I hope for. Focused on other issues, the hierarchy is unlikely to interfere with any cultural awakening. They won't even notice an artistic renascence until long after it is fully launched into the world.

The renewal of Catholic literature will happen—or fail to happen—through the efforts of writers. Culture is not an intellectual abstraction. It is human energy expressed through creativity, conversation, and community. Culture relies on individual creativity to foster consciousness, which then becomes expanded and refined through critical conversation. Those exchanges, in turn, support a community of shared values. The necessary work of writers matters very little unless it is recognized and supported by a community of critics, educators, journalists, and readers. The Communion of Saints is not only a theological concept, it is the model for a vibrant Catholic literary culture. There is so much Catholic literary talent—creative, critical, and scholarly—but most of it seems scattered and isolated. It lacks a vital sense of cultural community—specifically a conviction that together these individuals can achieve meaningful change in the world. If Catholic literati can recapture a sense of shared mission, the results would enlarge and transform literary culture.

If the state of contemporary Catholic literary culture can best be conveyed by the image of a crumbling, old, immigrant neighborhood, then let me suggest that it is time for Catholic writers and intellectuals to leave the homogenous, characterless suburbs of the imagination, and move back to the big city—where we can renovate these remarkable districts which have such grace and personality, such strength and tradition. It is time to renovate and reoccupy our own tradition. Starting the renovation may seem like a daunting task. But as soon as one place is rebuilt, someone else will already be at work next door, and gradually the whole city begins to reshape itself around you. Renovation is hard work, but what a small price to pay—to have the right home.

Sacred and Profane Love:
John Donne

I

Of all the great Christian poets of the British tradition, none is so joyfully and provocatively contradictory as John Donne. No other poet so renowned for his devotional writing, in both prose and verse, was also a master of love poetry, and certainly no English poet of such dark spiritual intensity ever showed such an irresistible sense of humor when the subject shifted from theology to sex. Readers discover exquisite pleasures in the lofty works of John Milton, but they don't find many laughs. Pious George Herbert saw deeply into the heart and soul of man, but he had little to say about women and nothing whatsoever about sex, except as a minor and mostly theoretical temptation.

The seventeenth century was the great age of English religious poetry. The immense, often violent energy of the Protestant Reformation (and Catholic Counter-Reformation) animated British culture, and for two generations poetry became spirituality's most vivid form of articulation. Virtually every significant poet of the period expressed these religious passions in some form, but there also emerged a group of extraordinary writers whose primary poetic subject was Christian spiritual experience—most notably John Milton, George Herbert, Richard Crashaw, Henry Vaughan, Thomas Carew, Thomas Traherne, and John Donne. Never before or after, has British literature experienced such a concentration of genius in devotional Christian poetry.

The oddness of Donne's position in this devout company can be easily illustrated through an exercise in imaginary subtraction. If, for example, all of Milton's religious poetry had been lost, he would survive as the author of a few fine early poems, such as *L'Allegro* and *Il Penseroso*, and an elegant aristocratic entertainment, *Comus*, but he would not be recognizable as "Milton," the classic author of the complex, sublime, and magisterial high style. If one subtracted the devotional verse from the works of Herbert, there would be so little left that the author would disappear to posterity. To only a slightly lesser extent, the same holds true with Crashaw, Vaughan, Carew, and Traherne. But Donne would still rank as one of the great poets of the language solely on the basis of his amatory poetry.

What makes Donne's position as a major religious poet even more problematic is that his love poetry is so openly sexy. He abandoned the elegantly sublimated style of Petrarchan tradition, which employed exaggerated and generalized praise to celebrate the beauty and virtue of the beloved while decorously bemoaning her cruel chastity. Donne gives the reader the vivid impression of addressing real women with the unapologetic and undisguised intention of seducing them. There was a good and practical reason why the older Donne, the Dean of St. Paul's Cathedral and the most celebrated preacher in London, did not publish the poems of his youth. The works surely embarrassed him, all the more keenly because they were so memorably individual, and they would have scandalized the public.

Donne's poems have certainly dismayed many readers. Early commentators found his verse too difficult, too intellectual, too lascivious, or too clever. James I quipped that Donne's poems "are like the peace of God; they pass all understanding." John Dryden felt Donne's overly ingenious wit had been a terrible influence on the poets who followed him. Even Donne's meter was criticized. Ben Jonson, who knew and admired the poet, was so annoyed by Donne's rhythmic freedom that he grumbled, "Donne, for not keeping of accent, deserved hanging." While Donne's sermons continued to be read with admiration after his death, his poetry was not widely admired until the twentieth century. Through the advocacy of writers such as T. S. Eliot, Ezra Pound, and F. R. Leavis, Donne became prized as one of the greatest poets of the language — "the one English metaphysical poet," in Pound's words, "who towers above all the rest." His resulting stature can be measured by a reasonably objective standard. In William Harmon's 1990 calculation of the 100 most widely reprinted poems in English, John Donne outranked every other poet in the English language—even William Shakespeare.

Donne's case exemplifies the difficulty of defining and appraising Christian poetry. If we characterize "Christian poetry" narrowly as verse written about religious experience in general accordance with broad Christian dogma, there is an inherent tendency toward favoring work that is pious in tone, plain in language, and lofty in sentiment. If instead we define the term more loosely to include all verse written by professing Christians, it encompasses most of the Western tradition over the past two millennia. The term becomes too loose to be useful. A happy medium between the two extremes is hard to articulate except in specific cases that allow for considerations of the historical, cultural, and biographical context. As William Wordsworth asserted, poetry represents "the spontaneous overflow of powerful feelings," and those feelings often include religious sentiments, which need to be analyzed judiciously. Religious expressions are shaped by immense social pressure. Orthodox Christian societies generally prefer to find religious sentiment expressed in respectful and respectable ways. There is also a stubborn and mistaken conviction that, in a world of sinners, religious poetry should be written by saints. It is easier to celebrate the possession of sanctity than the difficult struggle towards it. These are the questions that make Donne's case so illuminating. The young Donne was no saint, and the older Donne knew it. That recognition animates, enlarges, and humanizes his religious poetry in remarkable ways.

II

John Donne was born in London in 1572, the son of a prosperous ironmonger. The family remained Catholic in a period when the religion was illegal in England. Family members had suffered imprisonment, exile, torture, even martyrdom. His devout mother, Elizabeth Heywood Donne, counted St. Thomas More among her relations. Her brother, Jasper Heywood (the first English translator of Seneca) led the secret Jesuit mission in England. Donne's father died in 1576 leaving his son a substantial inheritance of about £750. This money provided for Donne's education and early travel, but it was not enough to sustain him as a gentleman with a family.

At twelve Donne was sent to Oxford to study. The family wanted him to be educated without having to renounce his Catholicism. Oxford required students to take a Protestant oath at sixteen or be expelled, so the early matriculation was necessary. Accreditation was not the goal. No Catholic could take a degree at any age. A few years later Donne moved to Trinity College, Cambridge. The rules were slightly looser there, but it also prohibited anyone "of the Romish persuasion" from obtaining a degree. Donne reportedly left Cambridge by sixteen. He then traveled abroad, possibly with Jasper Heywood, to study surreptitiously at Catholic universities. In 1592 he was back in London entering Lincoln's Inn to read law.

An intelligent, well-educated, and talented young man of limited independent means, Donne now faced the challenge of making a successful public career in a society that blocked both professional advancement and religious freedom for Catholics. This situation led the poet to a series of surprising changes, not all of them voluntary. In 1593 Donne's only brother Henry was arrested for sheltering a priest. He was tortured and then died in prison. The priest William Harrington (whom the poet presumably knew) was disemboweled and then hung. These horrific events seem to have triggered a genuine crisis of faith in the poet. Shortly thereafter, the twenty-one-year-old Donne converted to the Church of England—to the dismay of his steadfastly Catholic family.

Donne's conversion might appear the calculated act of a practical young man eager for advancement and alarmed by his brother's death. If the conversion was expedient, however, it does not seem to have been insincere. The Catholic cult of martyrdom troubled Donne as a sort of theologically assisted suicide. In his family the topic had been much pondered. His mother took pride in the family's legacy of martyrs. He had also begun to dislike and distrust Jesuit intrigues against Elizabeth 1 and the Anglican Church that so often occasioned the arrests and executions.

Donne's embrace of the Established Church proved to be enduring. He considered High Church Anglicanism as the true "Catholic" Church stripped of its Romish overlays. Mixed motives are common things, even in matters of faith. Donne was a man of complex and oftentimes contradictory passions. His religious views were unusually ecumenical for his sectarian age. He never lost his essentially Catholic worldview, though he rejected specific doctrines. He admired aspects of Calvinism but detested the doctrine of predestination. For him, there was truth in both Geneva and Rome, but England's middle way represented the most trustworthy form of Christianity.

Most of Donne's early poetry is impossible to date with accuracy. It seems likely, however, that his love poetry was largely written during his years at Lincoln's Inn. Ben Jonson claimed Donne had written his best work by the age of twenty-five. Catholic or Protestant, the handsome, young Donne was reportedly "a great visitor to the ladies," a phrase which begs the question of exactly what sorts of ladies he visited. From the literary evidence, they do not seem to have been exclusively women of cloistered virtue. His poetry makes clear that his admiration for women was unabashedly sexual, though women never seem solely the object of physical desire. He addresses the beloved with intellectual and emotional arguments that demonstrate the highest regard for female intelligence. No Renaissance English poet displays a more modern sense of romantic love as a respectful and reciprocal affair of equals.

Donne was intent on making a political career at the royal court or in aristocratic circles. Military service was a prerequisite for political employment. Donne volunteered for the war with Spain and fought in British expeditions to Cadiz and the Azores. He returned to become secretary in 1598 to Sir Thomas Egerton, the Lord Keeper of the Great Seal, one of the most powerful men in England. This appointment provided exactly the promising connection Donne needed, but he soon destroyed his chance for advancement. In 1601 Donne secretly married Ann More, Lord Egerton's ward and niece. Upon discovery of this rash, romantic act, Donne was not only dismissed from office but also briefly imprisoned—the predicament that occasioned his famous remark, "John Donne, Ann Donne, Un-done."

The impulsive marriage thwarted the poet's ambitious hopes. He did not find regular employment for twelve years. He struggled with little success to support his growing family. (He and Ann eventually had seven surviving children.) The impecunious couple was compelled to live with Ann's relations. It was a bitter situation for a talented and ambitious man. As Sir Herbert Grierson remarked, Donne's life entered a period of "wearing poverty and humiliating dependence."

Donne still longed for a political career. He attended on powerful men, some of them disreputable. He wrote anti-Catholic pamphlets to demonstrate his loyalty. He penned verses in praise of potential patrons. He even served a term in Parliament. No preferment came. Something about Donne's personality or manner did not earn the trust of the tough-minded and suspicious men who ruled England. He may have seemed too intellectual. He almost certainly appeared too indiscreet and soft-hearted. The powerful did, however, enjoy his company, admire his intelligence, and respect his matured moral character. They suggested the usual course for such mental and moral talents, a career in the Church. Donne repeatedly resisted the invitations to an ecclesiastical vocation. Although deeply religious, he saw himself as a man of the world—a soldier, poet, and politician—not a parson. He also probably worried that "some irregularities" in his younger life were too visible for a clergyman, even if they had long been mended. Finally, King James told Donne directly that he would have no preferment except in the Church.

In January 1615, at the age of forty-three, John Donne was ordained an Anglican priest. Advancement came quickly. Donne was appointed as one of the 48 royal chaplains. The king also ordered Cambridge to award the new priest a doctorate. Dr. Donne was then made Reader in Divinity at Lincoln's Inn. He was soon awarded additional parishes. His income grew steadily with each appointment. Donne's newly secured happiness was soon destroyed when his wife, only thirty-three years old, died in childbirth. (It was Ann's twelfth delivery.) Despite their worldly troubles, the marriage had been a devoted union, and Ann's death left him depressed and reclusive. Donne lived another fourteen years, but he never remarried. Now ordained, he made a virtue of necessity and settled into his late vocation.

Preaching at Lincoln's Inn to a congregation of lawyers, Donne had the ideal audience—intelligent, learned, and highly verbal. Many members of the congregation had been, according to the poet's first biographer, Izaak Walton, "the companions and friends of his youth." Puritan simplicity was not for Donne. His sermons were elaborate and brilliantly argued performances full of passionate conviction, dramatic language, and ingenious invention. Sunday sermons in this period often lasted two hours, so sustaining a congregation's attention was no small challenge. Donne combined rhetorical mastery and theological prowess to admonish and inspire his congregations, and he delivered his sermons with a skill that became legendary.

Jacobean London was famous for the quality of its preachers. "This City," boasted Donne, "hath the ablest preaching Clergy of any City in Christendom." Donne eventually commanded three of the most influential venues—the Chapel Royal at Whitehall Palace, Lincoln's Inn, and St. Paul's Cathedral where he was appointed Dean in 1621. In Reformation England preachers were major public figures, and pulpits represented the nation's most important "mass media." Sermons were not only an influential literary form; they were also a popular one. Religious tracts and sermons were the best-selling category of Elizabethan and Jacobean books. Donne excelled on both the pulpit and the page. During the final decade of his life, the poet's health deteriorated, but his oratorical fame continued to grow. With the death of Bishop Lancelot Andrews in 1626, Donne became the preeminent preacher in England.

In 1623 Donne developed serious illness, a nearly fatal fever. During his confinement and recovery, he kept a sort of diary, which he polished and published the next year as *Devotions Upon Emergent Occasions*, a series of extraordinary meditations on sickness and mortality as central to human existence. *Devotions* stands as a classic of English Christian literature, one still quoted today, even by people who do not recognize Donne's name. Here is a short passage much admired by at least one American novelist.

> No Man is an Island, entire of itself; every man is a piece of the Continent, a part of the main; if a Clod be washed away by the Sea, Europe is the less, as well as if a Promontory were, as well as if a Manor of thy friend's, of thine own were; a man's death diminishes me because I am involved in Mankind; and therefore never send to know for whom the bell tolls; it tolls for thee.

By early 1631 Donne had become weak and wizened from what proved to be his final illness—almost certainly a form of cancer. He focused his diminishing energies on writing out old sermons from his notes. (One hundred sixty of his sermons have survived.) To the alarm of his friends, Donne accepted the annual invitation to preach in the royal court at Whitehall on the first Friday of Lent. With the King in attendance, the dying Dean of St. Paul's took the pulpit and delivered to an amazed congregation—for the first time from a prepared script—a sermon for his own funeral. Published as *Death's Duell*, this profound and passionate meditation on the inevitability of death and the promise of the resurrection showed a great preacher still fully in command of his genius, even if the speaker no longer trusted his memory to deliver it without a written text.

Donne then returned to his Deanery. He handled the business affairs for the next few weeks. He also supervised the preparation for his own funeral monument in the cathedral. Donne had fires lit in his office, stripped off his clothes, and wrapped his emaciated body in a burial shroud, so that the artist could make a sketch. He kept the harrowing portrait in his bedroom—a true *memento mori*. In his final days he continuously repeated the Lord's Prayer. On March 31, 1631, he died peacefully at the age of 59. His funeral monument was built according to his plan. It was one of the few objects in St. Paul's to escape the Great Fire of London in 1666. The stone effigy still stands in the Cathedral's south choir.

III

Donne is conventionally categorized as the central figure of Metaphysical Poetry, a seventeenth-century literary movement that also includes Andrew Marvell, Richard Crashaw, George Herbert, Thomas Traherne, and Henry Vaughan. The works of these writers characteristically employ elaborately extended metaphors, argumentative structure, and intellectual language. Donne himself would not have understood the label "Metaphysical Poetry," or imagined himself as part of a poetic fraternity. Originally coined by Samuel Johnson, the term "metaphysical poets" was not intended to be complimentary. Johnson considered the group stylistically pretentious and emotionally inert—too much wit and not enough genuine feeling. For the three centuries after Donne's death, his poems were generally considered overly intellectual and elaborate, when they were considered at all.

One reason that Donne's verse perplexed many early readers was the sheer novelty of his approach. There was nothing in Elizabethan love poetry or religious verse quite like Donne, not even in Shakespeare. Popular approval, however, was not Donne's objective. His work was aimed at a sophisticated coterie. Some younger poets such as Herbert and Marvell were deeply influenced by his example, though their admiration reflected minority opinion. There were never many contemporary readers in any event. Donne's poems circulated only in manuscript until after his death. It would have been unseemly for a gentleman to publish his poetry. In the Elizabethan era, literary manuscripts were mostly shared privately among small circles of friends and acquaintances. During Donne's lifetime only seven of his poems were published. Only two of those publications were authorized by him—his elaborate public elegies, the *Anniversaries*, written in memory of an aristocratic girl he had never met.

Donne's chief innovation was to create a dense and dynamic style charged with an intellectual energy far in excess of the period style. His language is intimate and colloquial, but never plain or simple. His colloquialism is the passionate speech of a learned and inventive man speaking to his equals. This quality of colloquial energy is demonstrated nowhere better than in the abrupt and unforgettable first lines that launch his poems in bursts of emotional and dramatic energy:

> For Godsake hold your tongue and let me love . . .
>
> When by thy scorn, O murderess, I am dead . . .
>
> Now that thou hast lov'd me one whole day . . .
>
> What if this present were the world's last night?

One might make the case that Donne's colloquial style was merely an extension of Shakespeare's intimate, if slightly more formal manner, in the *Sonnets*, which were probably written about the same time as Donne's love poems. But Donne added another quality, his most significant innovation—a relentlessly argumentative organization. Donne wrote love poetry as if it were a theological debate. Before Donne, English poetry tended to be elegantly linear. The poet introduced an engaging line of thought and developed it by elaborating the basic notion. There might be a single turn of mood or perspective, as in many of Shakespeare's sonnets, but elegantly sustaining an idea rather than dialectically transforming it defined successful poetic performance. In musical terms, one might say that Donne took the song-like form of the Renaissance English lyric and gave it a quality of symphonic development.

Donne's poems progress by passionately argued and ingeniously sustained logic (or at least apparent logic). When he introduces an idea, he will most likely modify, overturn, or expand it in a subsequent stanza. In so doing, Donne developed a formal procedure that gradually transformed the possibilities of English poetry—the notion that each stanza represents a new stage of a progressive argument. A single short lyric could now unfold a dramatic narrative as emotionally varied as a sonnet sequence. Reading the opening of a poem, one could no longer predict where it might end.

In addition to complex colloquial language and dynamic argumentative structure, Donne developed a third signature innovation, the so-called "metaphysical conceit" that so annoyed Dryden and Johnson. A conceit is essentially a fanciful image or analogy that is elaborately developed to point out a striking parallel between two seemingly dissimilar objects. It is a virtuosic image or analogy sustained with bravado—like a tenor holding a high C. An example of a conceit is the title creature in Donne's "The Flea," a tiny insect who eventually carries a large number of meanings. The flea is, by turns, a conquering lover, a pampered child, a symbol of matrimony, a martyr to love, and finally just a dead bug. Donne expertly uses mock logic, sham theology, and sly humor to create a charming argument for seduction, though the reader probably feels that the poet's objective is as much to amuse his lady as to bed her.

In these early love poems, Donne created the modern lyric poem. Until Donne (and to a lesser extent his contemporary Ben Jonson), English lyric poetry had consisted mostly of songs or long sequences of interrelated short poems such as sonnets. Lyric poetry was a minor mode compared to the more commodious forms of epic or dramatic verse. The idea of a complex, independent short lyric hardly existed. Breadth and complexity were achieved by grouping short lyrics together in quasi-narrative sonnet sequences. Lyric poems did not even have titles before Donne and Herbert's generation; they were known only by their first lines or some generic heading such as "sonnet" or "song." Basing his work on classical Latin models, especially Horace and Ovid, Donne developed a form of lyric poetry that presented intensely argued human dramas of high emotional significance. These early poems changed the course of English poetry.

IV

Although the term "Metaphysical Poetry" historically had nothing to do with the philosophical discipline from which it borrows its name, Donne's love poetry bears an interesting relation to Christian metaphysics. Among the traditional concerns of metaphysics have been the relationships between the body and the soul, the visible and the invisible elements of human existence, the fixed and mutable aspects of identity. Although Donne's amatory verse explores sexual love, the author seems unable to apprehend physical intimacy without craving the spiritual or to celebrate sexual consummation without also imagining sacramental union.

It is unknown for whom Donne wrote his love poems—assuming that they actually address real women rather than imaginary ones. Tradition tactfully assigns the most lascivious ones to an "earlier" mistress and the more romantic "later" ones to the woman who would become his wife. A close reading of the poems supports the plausibility of this theory, though the paucity of the objective evidence keeps exact dating hypothetical. There may be other possible arrangements and chronologies. Certainly most of the major poems, however lusty, also seem overtly matrimonial.

In "The Flea," for example, the insect having sucked and mingled the blood of both lovers, becomes a symbol of their destined matrimony:

> This flea is you and I, and this
> Our marriage bed, and marriage temple is;
> Though parents grudge, and you, we're met
> And cloistered in these living walls of jet.

Here Donne specifically identifies the sexual and physical (the *bed*) with the spiritual and sacramental (the *temple*). As he develops the conceit, Donne's speaker claims that through a sort of sacramental union, the flea, like husband and wife in Christian matrimony, is of one flesh with the lovers. The speaker's theological argument is not to be taken seriously, of course, and the woman soon dispatches the insect without worrying about the triple sins of murder, sacrilege, and suicide the speaker has facetiously enumerated. The poem is an elegant and ingenious fiction, but it is significant that even in advocating free love, Donne cannot depart from Christian matrimony as the ideal.

Throughout his love poems Donne uses religious ideas in astonishing and amusing ways. In "The Relic" the speaker plans to wear a bracelet of his lover's hair so that on the last day she will be forced to visit him to reclaim it for her resurrected body. Donne's theology is again dubious, but the sentiment is both charming and evocative. It takes poise and confidence to use Doomsday as a come-on. In "The Ecstasy" Donne's lovers become so rapt in one another's gaze that their two souls leave their respective bodies to merge into an "abler soul." Sexual love paradoxically creates a spiritual union that prefigures matrimony, and physical love transcends the limits of the flush that embodies it.

> To our bodies turn we then, that so
>   Weak men on love revealed may look;
> Love's mysteries in souls do grow,
>   But yet the body is his book.
> And if some lover, such as we,
>   Have heard this dialogue of one,
> Let him still mark us; he shall see
>   Small change when we're to bodies gone.

Physical love is never minimized in Donne's verse. His love poems display none of the sexual guilt and disgust so often apparent in Shakespeare's sonnets and late tragedies. While Shakespeare anatomized the unstable psychological power struggles of love—its obsessions, distortions, humiliations, and betrayals—Donne explored the spiritual side of the erotic impulse, compulsively transforming it into a form of heightened discovery.

In these remarkable early poems, Donne helped create the modern notion of romantic love as an elective affair of equals who achieve a transfiguring union at once emotional, intellectual, sexual, and spiritual. This essentially sacramental vision—sexual attraction as the path love journeys to transcend the limitations of corporal desire—forms the basis for some of Donne's most capacious and accomplished poems, such as "The Ecstasy," "The Canonization," and "A Valediction: Forbidding Mourning." This last poem, which Izaak Walton asserts was written for Ann when the poet was about to embark on a long journey, celebrates the mysterious refinement of true love deepened by marriage:

> Dull sublunary lovers' love
> (Whose soul is sense) cannot admit
> Absence, because it doth remove
> Those things which elemented it.
>
> But we by a love so much refined,
> That ourselves know not what it is,
> Inter-assurèd of the mind,
> Care less, eyes, lips, and hands to miss.
>
> Our two souls, therefore, which are one,
> Though I must go, endure not yet
> A breach, but an expansiòn,
> Like gold to airy thinness beat.

What began as physical desire to merge two bodies has now become something that makes even physical proximity unnecessary—a metaphysical notion if ever there was one.

V

If transfiguring love suggests the joyful correspondences between body and soul, human mortality raises the dark metaphysical issues of bodily decay and personal extinction. Even the Christian consolation of eternal life and bodily resurrection is hugely qualified by the possibility of damnation. "Thou has made me, and shall Thy work decay?" Donne asks in what is traditionally considered the first of the "Holy Sonnets." (The editions of 1633 and 1635 differ in ordering the poems.) Even the faithful encounter fear, pain, and doubt when facing death:

> I dare not move my dim eyes any way,
> Despair behind, and death before doth cast
> Such terror, and my feeble flesh doth waste
> By sin in it, which it towards hell doth weigh;

There are no greater or more harrowing Christian poems in English than Donne's "Holy Sonnets." Aggressively written with vivid images, incisive phrasing, and relentless rhythmic drive, the poems do not unfold in the smooth lines of most Renaissance sonnets. Instead, they push violently forward, twisting past line breaks, torturing syntax to recreate the agonized consciousness of a man confronting the Four Last Things: Death, Judgment, Heaven, and Hell. At the heart of their enormous power is Donne's uncensored and vulnerable humanity. Just as he stripped his fine clothes to expose his diseased and decaying body for his final portrait, so do the "Holy Sonnets" reveal a poet who bares his guilty terror in contemplating his own mortality and the repellant features of his naked psyche. Donne rejects the euphemisms, sentimentality, and comfortable consolation that weaken most Christian poetry about death.

When Lord David Cecil edited the first *Oxford Book of Christian Verse* in 1940 (a year when such a book bore a special significance), he surveyed the tradition from medieval to modern times and declared that Donne took first place among English Christian poets. Donne alone, Cecil declared, was "equally interesting as Christian and as poet." Donne found the doctrines of sin and expiation experienced in his own life and reacted to them with his whole self. By nature, Donne was "rancorous, proud, morbid, and sensual," all of which proved advantageous to him as a religious poet, as his soul strained "to transcend its fleshly tenement." Outlining this compelling judgment, Cecil surely had the "Holy Sonnets" in mind.

In his dark sonnets, Donne does not despair—at least in the strict theological sense—of salvation. He understands that sinfulness does not easily surrender to divine grace. Human depravity resists redemption. Nor can humanity will salvation; only God can bestow it. Salvific grace is an involuntary, even violent overpowering of the fallen and divided human will. In a poem that combines Catholic baroque violence and the Calvinist doctrine of total depravity, Donne describes redemptive grace as a violent assault:

> Batter my heart, three-personed God, for You
> As yet but knock, breathe, shine, and seek to mend;
> That I may rise and stand, o'erthrow me, and bend
> Your force to break, blow, burn, and make me new.

The metaphors ultimately become sexual—another feature of Catholic baroque style—in which the sinner "betrothed to your enemy" can only be divorced from evil by being overpowered by divine grace. This is no gentle vision of redemption. It marks a life and death struggle with immortal stakes.

Not all of Donne's religious poetry is dark and violent. Much is quiet, humble, and compassionate. In "The Litany" the poet addresses the Trinity first separately and then together, with hopeful assurance of their grace, but he never loses his awareness of the consequences of original sin. To his inherently fallen nature, the poet realizes he has added his own voluntary sins—"being sacrilegiously / Half wasted with youth's fires, of pride and lust." Even in his gentle prayer, "A Hymn to God the Father," which Donne had set to music and sung at St. Paul's, the poet addresses the deity with a catalogue of his own unworthiness:

> Wilt Thou forgive that sin where I begun,
>> Which was my sin, though it were done before?
> Wilt Thou forgive that sin, through which I run,
>> And do run still: though still I do deplore?
>>> When Thou hast done, Thou hast not done,
>>>> For I have more.

Donne has put his literary bravura aside in this poem of humble supplication. One might not even recognize the hymn as the work of the same verbal virtuoso who wrote "The Flea" or "The Ecstasy," were it not for the repeated pun on the poet's name. The hymn's key phrase, "When Thou hast done," also implies "When God finally has Donne in death and eternity." The poet knows that the Lord will appreciate the cleverly sustained pun in a poem purportedly expressing the supplicant's absolute surrender to divine grace because if Donne does not also offer his verbal genius, then God does not truly have all of him.

Donne understood the contradictory complexities of his own life with its dynamic and unexpected course—a Catholic, an Anglican, a courtly libertine, a devoted husband, a soldier, a lawyer, a theologian, a failed politician, a father, a reluctantly ordained cleric, a tortured widower, a preacher of genius, a pious priest haunted by his own unworthiness, and a great poet who almost entirely abandoned his art in later years and came to regret some of the finest poems ever written in English. "When Thou hast done," indeed. Who but God could possess all of such a man?

God's Grandeur:
Gerard Manley Hopkins

I

If modern Christian poetry has a saint, it is Gerard Manley Hopkins. No other poet, at least in English, occupies such a lofty position in terms of both literary achievement and spiritual authority. Other major religious poets—T. S. Eliot, W. H. Auden, Geoffrey Hill, Richard Wilbur—have their work studied with respect. In Hopkins's case, the life has been canonized along with the writing. His reputation transcends questions of purely literary merit. He is venerated as a figure of sanctity, redemptive suffering, and heroic virtue.

Hopkins is a singular figure in other ways. No other poet in English has achieved such major status with so small a body of writing. His mature work consists of only forty-nine poems—none of which he saw published in his lifetime. Even when one adds the two dozen early poems written at Oxford and various fragments found in notebooks after his death, his literary oeuvre is meager in size, even for a writer who died in his forties.

Yet Hopkins ranks as one of the most frequently reprinted poets in English. In William Harmon's statistical survey of anthologies and textbooks, *The Top 500 Poems* (1992), Hopkins stood in seventh place among all English-language poets—surpassed only by William Shakespeare, John Donne, William Blake, Emily Dickinson, W. B. Yeats, and William Wordsworth (all prolific and longer-lived writers). Universally taught, Hopkins's poetry has inspired a mountain of scholarly commentary. Despite the difficulty of his style, he is also popular among students.

Invisible in his own lifetime, Hopkins now stands as a major poetic innovator who, like Walt Whitman or Emily Dickinson, prefigured the Modernist revolution. A Victorian by chronology, Hopkins belongs by sensibility to the twentieth century—an impression strengthened by the odd fact that his poetry was not published until 1918, twenty-nine years after his death. No one would have predicted the poet's exalted position when the first edition was published, especially not its editor Robert Bridges. He had waited until old age and his appointment as Poet Laureate to release his late friend's work. He feared that readers would ridicule Hopkins's unconventional and idiosyncratic verse. Even then his introduction apologized for the poet's "Oddity and Obscurity." His worries proved groundless. The new century was ready for Hopkins's oddity. His posthumous legacy soon changed the course of modern poetry, influencing leading writers such as W. H. Auden, Dylan Thomas, Robert Lowell, John Berryman, Ted Hughes, Geoffrey Hill, and Seamus Heaney.

Among the great Christian poets of the modern era, Hopkins is unique in that his verse is almost entirely religious in subject and perspective. A devout and orthodox Catholic convert who became a Jesuit priest, he considered poetry a spiritual distraction unless it could serve his faith. This quality makes his popularity in our secular and often anti-religious age seem paradoxical. Yet the devotional nature of his work may actually be responsible for his continuing readership. Hopkins's passionate Catholicism provides something not easily found elsewhere in the current curriculum—serious and disciplined Christian spirituality.

The history of English poetry is inextricably linked to Christianity. As Donald Davie commented in his introduction to *The New Oxford Book of Christian Verse* (1981), "Through most of the centuries when English verse has been written, virtually all of the writers of that verse quite properly and earnestly regarded themselves as Christian." Not all poetry was overtly religious, but Christian beliefs and perspectives shaped its imaginative and moral vision. The tradition of explicitly religious poetry, however, was both deep and continuous. Starting with Chaucer, Langland, and the anonymous medieval authors of *The Pearl* and *Sir Gawain and the Green Knight*,

Christianity emerged early as a central element of English literature. The tradition continued robustly for six centuries with major poets in every generation—John Donne, George Herbert, Henry Vaughan, John Milton, William Blake, William Wordsworth, Alfred Tennyson, Christina Rossetti, and both Brownings, as well the great hymnodists, Isaac Watts, William Cowper, and Charles Wesley. Then midway in the nineteenth century, the tradition founders.

Victorian writers experienced a crisis of faith as they tried to re-concile modern science and philosophy with religious tradition. Matthew Arnold's melancholy masterpiece of anguished Victorian agnosticism, "Stanzas from the Grande Chartreuse" (1855), articu-lates the broad spiritual dilemma. Entering the ancient Alpine monastery, Arnold contrasts the millennium of faith it represents with his own powerful but unsatisfying rationalism. He describes his intellectual and emotional dilemma as "Wandering between two worlds, one dead, / The other powerless to be born." This uneasy and unsatisfying uncertainty offered little peace in either direction. Accepting faith, many were full of doubt. Rejecting faith, they experienced an existential emptiness.

Significantly, it was during this moment of pervasive religious skep-ticism and spiritual anxiety that Hopkins emerged to transform and renew the tradition of Christian poetry. Consequently, he occupies a strangely influential position in the history of English-language religious poetry. He possessed the special power of a writer who was simultaneously both inside and outside the cultural mainstream. As an Oxford-educated Anglican, trained in the classics, he exemplified elite British culture. As a Catholic convert and Jesuit priest, he stood outside social and intellectual respectability. To borrow Arnold's image, Hopkins had wandered between two worlds but had found the power to renew the ancient vision. His audaciously original style not only swept away the soft and sentimental conventions of nineteenth-century religious verse, it also provided a vehicle strong enough to communicate the overwhelming power of his faith. His small body of work—hidden for years—provided most of the elements out of which modern Christian poetry would be born.

II

Gerard Manley Hopkins was born in Stratford, Essex in 1844, the eldest of nine children in a prosperous and cultured family. His father Manley Hopkins worked as a marine insurance adjustor, but he also wrote poetry, criticism, and even a history of Hawaii. His mother Kate Hopkins, a devout woman, loved music and poetry. The family brimmed with artists. Two of the brothers became painters. One sister composed music. Another wrote poetry. The parents were moderate Anglicans, following a middle course between the High Church Anglo-Catholics and Low Church Evangelicals. The family religious atmosphere was powerful and genuine. Not only did Gerard become a Jesuit priest, his eldest sister Miriam entered an Anglican convent.

As with many poets and priests, the singular qualities of Hopkins's character emerged early. At Highgate, the North London public school Hopkins attended for eight years, the young poet was notably upright and industrious. He also demonstrated an ascetic strain, once going without liquids for a week. Too delicate for sports, he excelled in academics. He won the School Poetry Prize and, in his final year, the gold medal as Highgate's most distinguished student. Despite his scholastic success, Hopkins was unhappy at Highgate. "I had no love for my schooldays," he later wrote, "and wished to banish the remembrance of them."

In 1863 the nineteen-year-old Hopkins entered Balliol College, Oxford to read Classics. Here he found a congenial and stimulating new home. Balliol was Oxford's most rigorous college. Benjamin Jowett, the celebrated University Professor of Greek, became Hopkins's first tutor. In 1866 the role passed to Walter Pater, future prophet of the Aesthetic Movement. Among the other intellectual attractions of Oxford was Matthew Arnold, then in his second term as Oxford Professor of Poetry—the first holder of the chair to lecture in English rather than Latin. At Oxford Hopkins made many lifelong friends, most notably Robert Bridges, who later became Poet

Laureate. Bridges's artistic fellowship and personal affection sustained Hopkins in life and, after death, saved his work from oblivion.

Hopkins wrote poetry at Oxford, but his great intellectual passion was theology. Oxford was still an exclusively Anglican institution with compulsory chapel and staffed by celibate clergymen. Underneath the official unanimity, however, religious debates seethed and periodically exploded. At stake was the future of the Church of England, which in 1832 had become partially separated from the state. The political change raised issues about the theological, liturgical, and ecclesiastical identity of Anglicanism. The Tractarians, who would come to be known as the Oxford Movement, argued that Anglicanism was the true "catholic church," a correct middle way between the errors of Roman Catholicism and the excess of Protestant reforms. The Church of England, they asserted, needed to revive its older liturgical and theological traditions. The Tractarian viewpoint was rejected both by Low Church Evangelicals and Broad Church liberals. The Evangelicals remained proudly Protestant, suspicious of Roman ritual, and strict in their literal adherence to scripture. The Broad Church advocates, who represented much of the Anglican elite, hoped to reconcile Christianity with modern secular thought by being flexible on dogma and minimizing the supernatural aspects of the faith. Christianity need not, they felt, always be taken too literally. At the far end of the liberal wing, Anglicanism had already merged into the genteel and cultured agnosticism that allowed Arnold to predict that poetry would replace religion as humanity's means to interpret life and develop its higher potential.

Hopkins responded to the intellectual excitement and spiritual urgency of these theological debates. He attended High Church services and lectures, finding himself drawn to the devotional rituals revived by Anglo-Catholics. He shared the Tractarian longing for an apostolic and undivided Christian church. The Oxford Movement had already become notorious among Anglicans because so many Tractarians had converted to Roman Catholicism—most notably John Henry Newman. The Anglican establishment scorned these Roman converts, often referring to them as "perverts."

Slowly but ineluctably Hopkins followed the same spiritual path as so many members of the Oxford Movement. In July 1866, he decided to join the Roman Church. He resolved to keep the matter private until he finished his degree, but he wrote to Newman for advice. When they finally met in September, the cardinal declared that Hopkins needed to inform his parents before being received into the church. The nervous son waited until the last moment to write his father. The family replied with shock, sorrow, and angry disapproval. A week later Newman accepted Hopkins into the Catholic Church. His parents did not banish their Roman son, but their previously warm relationship turned tense. His father would disinherit Hopkins when he was ordained.

Meanwhile Hopkins triumphantly finished his exams in Greek and Latin. Not only did he gain a first-class degree, he scored the highest of any student. After a short holiday, Hopkins began teaching in Newman's oratory school in Birmingham. Victorian Catholic institutions were shabby and precarious enterprises. The Church had barely begun to rebuild its presence in Britain after centuries of prohibition. The congregations were mostly poor Irish immigrants. Hopkins found teaching exhausting and unrewarding, a situation exacerbated by his physical fragility and nervous sensitivity. (Scholars now believe the poet suffered from Crohn's disease—a slow, painful, potentially fatal condition.) His unhappiness did not cool his spiritual ardor. In Birmingham, Hopkins resolved to become a priest. He had originally planned to be an Anglican clergyman, so the new vocation was hardly surprising. His decision, however, to join the Society of Jesus, a religious order long and deeply distrusted by English Protestants, alienated many friends and teachers.

Hopkins's conversion marked the great turning point in his life and not in just a spiritual sense. His entry into Roman Catholicism and the Jesuit order transformed his personal, social, and artistic identity. A serious academic career was no longer open to him. There were no positions for a Catholic at Oxford or Cambridge, and no endowed livings for Roman priests. Many friendships ended. His Tractarian mentor, Edward Pusey, refused to meet with the "pervert." Hopkins had thrived in the cultured atmosphere of Balliol. He was not temperamentally suited to the drudgery of slum ministry or basic schoolwork. He was a saintly aesthete caught in an activist life. His spiritual resolve and discipline were absolute, but the flesh and nerves were weak. Alienated from family and friends, Hopkins was frequently lonely and depressed. From one of his early assignments, he expressed what would become habitual complaints:

> I am very anxious to get away from this place. I have become very weak in health . . . Teaching is very burdensome, especially when you have much of it.

His priestly vocation also overwhelmed his poetic identity. Hopkins saw no role for poetry in his new life. He embraced the Catholic notion, especially strong among Jesuits, that personal ambition must be sacrificed to free the spirit to do God's work and serve others. A literary career conflicted with the unqualified spiritual dedication necessary to be a priest. A young man of immense intellectual ambition, Hopkins not only renounced his art but actually destroyed his early verses as a symbol of his dedication (though not before sending his friend Bridges copies). As Hopkins later confided to the poet-parson Richard Watson Dixon, "What I had written I burnt before I became a Jesuit and resolved to write no more, as not belonging to my profession." For the next seven years the seminarian maintained a poetic silence.

When Hopkins joined the Society of Jesus in 1868, he was twenty-four years old. He would spend the remaining twenty years of his life in the tightly knit and demanding order organized by Ignatius of Loyola on a military model to train "soldiers of God." Jesuit priests are not ordained until they are thirty-three. Hopkins spent two years as a novitiate at Manresa House in Rochampton. (Manresa was named after the cave outside Barcelona where St. Ignatius first formulated his Spiritual Exercises.) He then devoted three years of philosophical study at St. Mary's Hall, Stonyhurst. He returned to Manresa for a year to teach before going to St. Beuno's College in

North Wales in final training for his ordination. He was happy at St. Beuno's studying and praying in the beautiful Welsh countryside.

Hopkins's self-imposed silence was finally broken in 1875—two years before his ordination—when he read about the deadly wreck of the German ship the *Deutschland*. Among the many victims were five Franciscan nuns who had been exiled from Prussia when the German Empire expelled all Catholic clergy and confiscated church property. The Rector at St. Beuno's had remarked that someone should write a poem about the incident. Hopkins eagerly asked permission to do so. What emerged was an intricate, innovative, and visionary 280-line *tour de force* "The Wreck of the Deutschland"—a poem so strange and explosively original that none of its early readers could understand it. The editor of the Jesuit journal *The Month* had initially encouraged the project, but he eventually rejected the poem as unintelligible. Bridges disliked it so much he later referred to Hopkins's formidable first mature poem as "the dragon folded at the gate to forbid all entry." Hopkins hopefully sent *The Month* another poem, which was also rejected. He then stopped seeking publication. But writing the poems had proved decisive. Reawakened by his visionary composition, Hopkins considered his private vow of literary silence lifted.

Hopkins spent most of his life in exclusively male institutions from public school and university to seminary and rectory. There has been scholarly speculation that he had a homosexual orientation. If so, his inclination posed no obstacle to his vocation. Hopkins was almost certainly a lifelong celibate, and he treated all of his vows—poverty, chastity, and obedience—with earnest dedication.

The question of Hopkins's sexuality, however, seems less mysterious than his sudden transformation from an ordinary poet into a bard of luminous originality. There was no period of apprenticeship in his poetic development—just an explosion from silence into greatness. This creative metamorphosis surely began in his quiet years of religious formation as a novice immersed in Ignatian spiritual practice. The goal of Jesuit discipline is not artistic, but it does deliberately develop the powers of imagination. The Spiritual Exercises, for example, ask the novice to visualize himself in episodes from the life of Christ so that body and soul, emotions and intellect are fully engaged in the meditation—a poetic rather than analytical form of prayer. In his long silent and solitary retreats, Hopkins grew and deepened his spiritual capacity in exactly the ways his spiritual directors intended. But somehow in Hopkins's singular case, the training also focused and intensified his poetic talents into genius.

In 1877, as he approached ordination, Hopkins experienced a joyful surge of inspiration. In quick succession he created half a dozen of his most famous poems—"God's Grandeur," "The Starlit Night," "Spring," "The Windhover," "Pied Beauty," and "Hurrahing the Harvest." These magnificent sonnets resembled "The Wreck of the Deutschland" in style, but the texture was less opaque and the manner more direct. Without losing any of his strange originality, Hopkins made his work more accessible. These modern psalms celebrate the divine glory of creation in language and images that feel startlingly fresh and tangibly immediate:

> Glory be to God for dappled things—
>   For skies of couple-colour as a brinded cow;
>   For rose-moles all in stipple upon trout that swim;
>   Fresh-firecoal chestnut-falls; finches' wings

His return to poetry was triumphant, though entirely private. Perhaps recognition might eventually arrive. His creative breakthrough and rapid artistic growth seemed to promise a prolific and satisfying literary career.

The Society of Jesus develops its priests by rotating them through various assignments in different locations. After ordination, Hopkins moved repeatedly—to parishes in Sheffield, London, Oxford, Liverpool, Manchester, and Glasgow. He had neither the aptitude nor the energy for parish work, especially in the urban slums the Jesuits mostly served. At St. Beuno's his practice sermon caused uproarious laughter. His fellow Jesuits liked Hopkins, but they viewed the devout young priest as frail, nervous, and eccentric. His superiors had no notion how to use his talents. After half a dozen short and unsuccessful pastoral postings, they decided he should teach. How could they not admire his distinguished classical scholarship? For the rest of his life, Hopkins was doomed to the uncongenial job of schoolmaster.

In 1884 Hopkins moved to his last assignment in Dublin. His new position had a resonant title, Professor of Greek at University College, Dublin, and Fellow of the Royal University of Ireland. The reality of his situation was less impressive. Lacking financial endowment or academic distinction, the college was the dilapidated remnant of Newman's plan for a Catholic Irish University. The buildings were in poor repair. The library's books had been appropriated by a seminary. Course offerings were limited. The University College existed mostly to grade examinations and issue degrees for other institutions.

In Dublin, Hopkins lectured on Greek literature. His teaching was no more successful than his sermons. His classes were noisy and unruly. To the irritation of his students, he did not teach the material that would appear on the exams. They treated the meek English priest with intentional rudeness. His chief responsibility, however, was to grade examinations sent in six times each year by colleges associated with the university—sometimes five hundred in a batch. He did the burdensome work meticulously, but he hated the repetitious and exacting toil.

Hopkins felt a growing isolation in Ireland. "To seem the stranger lies my lot, my life / Among strangers," he wrote in a late sonnet. His life had indeed become a series of interlocking estrangements. His faith had separated him from his family and Oxford community. His religious devotion and physical frailty had prevented him from achieving his scholarly and artistic aspirations. Now an Englishman among Irish Catholics seething for independence, he felt always the uneasy outsider—a royalist among republicans.

A painful and constant conflict characterized Hopkins's life as a priest. His native sensitivity and individualistic artistic personality made it difficult to meet the practical and communal responsibilities of a Jesuit. It was not a matter of faith or dedication. By every account, Hopkins led a life of sacrifice and sanctity. His letters and journals, however, show how unequal he felt to the heroic Jesuit vision of the priesthood. "I have never wavered in my vocation," Hopkins wrote Dixon, "but I have not lived up to it." "Do you want to become a great saint?" Ignatius of Loyola declared, "Ask God to send you many sufferings." Hopkins's physical pain and emotional anguish were real and constant. He accepted those burdens willingly, but they nonetheless exacted a heavy physical and mental price.

A sense of failure pervades Hopkins's final years. After his early triumphs as "the star of Balliol," he had stumbled in his subsequent endeavors—parish work, preaching, scholarship, teaching, and poetry. He was both driven and tortured by his longing for self-perfection. Despite his considerable spiritual discipline, he could not shed the ordinary human craving for public achievement and recognition. Spiritual lives are rarely simple or static, and it is important not to reduce Hopkins to either a suffering neurasthenic or a pious anchorite. Human nature is not binary. An ascetic feels the hungers he denies. Artistic genius craves recognition. Both priest and poet, Hopkins carried the weight of both vocations on his frail frame.

In 1885, the despondency and isolation of the Dublin period found artistic expression in another intense and private burst of creativity. The new poems—once again a series of sonnets—were as dark and desolate as the earlier St. Beuno's sonnets were radiantly joyful. Hopkins mentioned their creation to Bridges in a letter (but did not send the poems): "Four of these came like inspirations unbidden and against my will." When Bridges found the verses among his friend's posthumous papers, he called them the "terrible sonnets" (the adjective refers to the terror they convey). The poems violently portray the anguish and self-contempt he felt at the failures and renunciations of his life, and his near despair at the spiritual impasses of his inner life.

No worst, there is none. Pitched past pitch of grief,
More pangs will, schooled at forepangs, wilder wring.
Comforter, where, where is your comforting?

In Dublin Hopkins's health worsened. His eyesight grew weak. He was frequently depressed. He continued to write in brief intervals of energy and concentration. His last poems often reach toward a new simplicity without losing their rich musicality and spiritual weight.

Thou art indeed just, Lord, if I contend
With thee; but, sir, so what I plead is just.
Why do sinners' ways prosper? and why must
Disappointment all I endeavour end?

In 1889 Hopkins contracted typhoid fever. His condition deteriorated. He developed peritonitis. He was given last rites. His superiors asked the poet's family to come from England. They stood by their forty-four-year-old son as he died. His final words were, "I am so happy. I am so happy." The order buried him in Glasnevin Cemetery in an unmarked grave among his brother Jesuits. Bridges quickly arranged to save the poet's manuscripts and papers. The Highgate School published a generous and respectful obituary of their alumnus. It praised his character and scholarship. It made no mention of his poetry.

III

"No doubt my poetry errs on the side of oddness," Hopkins wrote to Bridges. No reader is likely to disagree. Hopkins's poetry is so distinctively original and idiosyncratic that it resembles nothing else in the English canon. Although he was a Victorian poet, he does not sound like any of his contemporaries—nor any of ours. Hopkins did not build on conventional foundations of English verse. He reinvented the art from the ground up in terms of meter, syntax, and texture.

The distinctive sound and style of Hopkins's poetry comes primarily from two elements—its dense concentration of musical effects and its powerful but irregular rhythms. Poets use the physical sound of words for musical effect, but no poet before Hopkins (and few after him) packed so many sound effects so tightly together. Most poetry reads like heightened speech. Meter, word play, and figurative language intensify language in ways native speakers recognize as verse rather than prose or ordinary speech. Hopkins's poetry, however, often sounds like a different order of language altogether—poetry heightened beyond the normal limits of poetry. He fashioned a new kind of verse which expressed passionate emotions in a great welter of rhythmic word music and figurative language.

Here is a single sentence from Hopkins, the opening line of "The Windhover," a poem which bears the subtitle "To Christ our Lord":

> I caught this morning morning's minion, king-
> > dom of daylight's dauphin, dapple-dawn-drawn Falcon, in his riding
> > Of the rolling level underneath him steady air, and striding
> High there, how he rung upon the rein of a wimpling wing
> In his ecstasy! then off, off forth on swing,
> > As a skate's heel sweeps smooth on a bow-bend: the hurl and gliding
> > Rebuffed the big wind.

These ecstatic lines are so dense that it is difficult for a first-time reader to know exactly what the author intends to convey. The title states the poem is about a falcon, so it is easy to construe the lines as describing a raptor in the morning sky. The poem's subtitle suggests, however, that the bird also bears a relation to Christ. The nature of that relation remains mysterious, though the falcon radiates more than natural significance. But what does the first-time reader do with all the descriptive phrases that keep the sentence running for nearly seven lines? The meaning of the grammatical interlocked phrases requires both study and speculation. There is, however, no mistaking the elaborate word music in "The Windhover." The lines employ alliteration, rhyme (including internal rhyme), assonance, and repetition. The first two lines contain more alliteration than most poems: "morning morning's minion" followed by "dom of daylight's dauphin, dapple-dawn-drawn." Hopkins unabashedly reiterates his consonants—six *d*-sounds in a row in line two. He even combines individual words into alliterative compounds such as "dapple-dawn-drawn."

Hopkins's verse also moves oddly. Not only do the lines run into one another, but some lines break in the middle of words ("king- / dom"). The first line has ten syllables as befits a sonnet, but it achieves the meter by breaking the final word in half with the rhyme "king" calling attention to the strange disruption. Things only get stranger as the poem proceeds. The next two lines each have sixteen syllables and the fourth line has thirteen, still managing to spill over. An English sonnet conventionally has forty syllables in the first four lines; "The Windhover" has fifty-five.

Poetic form takes tangible elements in a language—things which native speakers can easily hear—and arranges them for expressive effect. In traditional English poetry, poets took speech stress and syllable count and linked them into fixed ratios creating our standard meters such as iambic pentameter—ten syllables that alternate unstressed and stressed syllables in a one-to-one ratio. (This is the famous dee-DUM-dee-DUM-dee-DUM-dee-DUM-dee-DUM intoned by generations of high school teachers). To link the individual lines and add a sense of closure, poets added rhymes at the ends of lines. The artistic goal was generally to give language a regular, mesmerizing swing.

Here is Hopkins's most popular contemporary, Alfred Tennyson, writing in iambic pentameter with his customary lyric elegance. Note how smoothly the rhythm unfolds in perfectly balanced phrases. Each of these lines has ten syllables with five stresses in each line, all arranged in a symmetrical alternating pattern:

˘   /   ˘   / ˘ / ˘   / ˘ /

Now sleeps the crimson petal, now the white:

˘   / ˘ / ˘ / ˘ / ˘ /

Nor waves the cypress in the palace walk;

The fundamental driving force of Hopkins's poem was a new rhythmic form he called "sprung rhythm," which Hopkins claimed had been "haunting his ear so he put it on paper." Sprung rhythm "consists in scanning by accents or stresses alone," he explained, "without any account of the number of syllables." Although his system may sound abstract, it works by exactly the same rules that rap poets developed over a century later.

Here is the opening of Hopkins's sonnet "Pied Beauty," notated to mark the places which Hopkins probably heard the beats:

/   /   /   /   /

Glory be to God for dappled things—

/   /   /   /   /

For skies of couple-colour as a brinded cow;

Each line has five stresses, but the number of syllables is irregular—nine in one line, twelve in the other.

If Hopkins's lines are initially hard to understand, one can feel the power of their emotion overflowing to use his own religiously loaded term "in his ecstasy." Publishing Hopkins's poetry for the first time, Bridges apologized for their "Oddity and Obscurity." That obscurity may hinder some readers, but the density of Hopkins's language serves the function of slowing the reader down to look at each line more closely.

Hopkins's poetic style and versification are entirely original. There is nothing in earlier English that sounds quite like his poetry, except isolated lines from Shakespeare and Milton. Nonetheless it is easy to identify various individual elements he borrowed from tradition—the rhythms of nursery rhymes and oral ballads, the alliterative beat of Anglo-Saxon verse, the sinuous lineation and syntax of late Milton, Welsh chiming rhymes, and the flexible word order of Latin and Greek poetry. What isn't easy is to understand how he combined these incongruous elements to create compelling and coherent new structures of sounds.

The oddness and originality of Hopkins's poetry comes mostly from its basis in pure sound. At Oxford he became interested in music. He learned to play the violin and piano. Later he even composed a few songs. Hopkins was only an amateur musician, but his lifelong passion for the art reflected his fascination with sound. He claimed his poems were written for the ear and not for the eye. Sprung verse came to him as "a new rhythm" he heard in his auditory imagination. The page, like a musical score, was the transcription of that verbal music. However modern Hopkins's poetry appears on the page, it is also radically ancient—not traditional but primal. Hopkins returned poetry to its oral and performative roots.

The last of the Victorian poets, the first of the Modernists, the idiosyncratic loner working outside literary history—no single category seems adequate to explain Hopkins. As he pressed forward into the future, he also reached back in time—to find both the living roots of Christianity and English poetry. His art was his account of a spiritual journey that had nothing to do with secular notions of progress or tradition. Any assessment of Hopkins that fails to engage in the authenticity of that interior odyssey will miss why his poetry matters so deeply to his readers. They feel the reality of a journey, to quote T. S. Eliot, towards "A condition of complete simplicity / (Costing not less than everything)." Hopkins wagered his life as the stakes for this exploration. The poems are the log of that journey as he moved through ecstasy and desolation toward his ineffable destination.

Two Poets Named Dunstan Thompson

To sing is the work of a lover.
ST. AUGUSTINE

Like most poets, Dunstan Thompson has been neglected. His early work has been out of print for seventy years. His later work appeared only in a posthumous edition that was never commercially distributed. No current anthologies reprint his poems. His critical prose has never been collected. His novel and travel book have become items for antiquarian booksellers. Although Thompson enjoyed considerable fame in the 1940s, his reputation evaporated within his own lifetime. Until D. A. Powell and Kevin Prufer compiled their tribute volume, *Dunstan Thompson: On the Life & Work of a Lost American Master* (2010), one might have said that the author had been entirely forgotten. Even now most poetry readers will not recognize his name.

Thompson, however, is a neglected poet with a difference. Despite his obscurity, he has managed to generate controversy. Invisible in the broader culture, he has attracted a fitful audience, though few — both enthusiastic and openly partisan. In the forty years since his death in 1975, Thompson's work has continued to be read and discussed among poetic coteries in both England and America, though their commentary has rarely appeared in print. The people who care about his legacy have known it is good enough to argue about.

Two contradictory views of Thompson and his poetry have emerged, which seem to reflect an irreconcilable dichotomy inherent in both his life and work. Each faction has made exclusive claim to his legacy. For one group, Thompson stands as a pioneering poet of gay experience and sensibility. He was one of the first poets — and certainly the best of the World War II era—to write openly about homosexual experience. Although his language remained slightly coded—even straight sex could not be depicted literally at that time without censorship or prosecution—there was little ambiguity about the hidden world of casual sexual encounters he describes so powerfully in his neo-romantic and rhapsodic poems. An heir to Walt Whitman and Hart Crane, Thompson stands, to quote Jim Elledge, as "a kindred soul" to contemporary gay poets.

To the second group, Thompson ranks as one of the important English-language Catholic poets of the twentieth century. A neo-classical writer of cosmopolitan sensibility, he cultivated an austere and formal style to explore themes of history, culture, and religion. In ways that seem more European than American, the mature Thompson also used the long perspectives of Christian and Classical history to understand the modern world after the devastations, dislocations, and atrocities of a troubled century.

There is no question that Thompson's poetry falls into two parts— the early work published during the 1940s and the later work gath-ered posthumously in 1984. (There is no discernible middle period since Thompson published mainly prose in the decade after the war.) Each period presents a very different sense of the author—two divergent voices and concerns. Each period also employs a radically different style. The early verse is expansive, ornate, dramatic, and confessional. The later poetry is austere, urbane, controlled, and quietly confident. One cannot confuse the two styles, but is style the full measure of the man? Are there really two different Dunstan Thompsons? Does the youthful romantic really have so little in common with the mature classicist? Does admiring the poetry of one period prevent an appreciation of the other?

The controversy over Thompson's legacy has been further exagger-ated by the fact that many commentators have read only part of the author's work and know only fragments of his life. Such ignorance is hardly surprising given the difficulty and expense of obtaining Thompson's books and the lack of reliable information about his life. There are no collected poems, no published letters, and no biography. The author himself complicated the situation because he so strongly preferred his later work that he declined to have his early poems reprinted—"a waste of youth," he called them. His literary executor and surviving partner Philip Trower has respected that request until now. The long overdue publication of Thompson's selected poems, edited by Gregory Wolfe in 2015, finally provides the opportunity to see this fascinating author's poetry in perspective.

II

I was not yet in love, yet I loved to love.
ST. AUGUSTINE

Dunstan Thompson was born in New London, Connecticut, in 1918. His father was a naval officer who was frequently at sea. His mother was a shy, religious woman who was impractical with money. An only child, Thompson travelled extensively with his mother, once even visiting Panama when his father was stationed in the Canal Zone. Growing up mostly in Annapolis, Maryland, Thompson attended half a dozen Catholic schools before entering Harvard in 1936. He was a conspicuously sophisticated and literary undergraduate who wrote for the *Harvard Monthly* and spent one summer in England as a private student of the poet Conrad Aiken. In 1939 Thompson left Harvard probably to avoid being expelled for bad grades. By then he had not only discovered his poetic ambitions but also his homosexuality.

Using a legacy from his aunt, Thompson moved to New York where he and his fellow Harvard poet and drop-out, Harry Brown, published *Vice Versa*, an ambitious and irreverent small magazine. (Brown would become a best-selling novelist and Academy Award-winning screenwriter.) Lasting only three issues, *Vice Versa* presented work by W. H. Auden, Ezra Pound, Dylan Thomas, Weldon Kees, and Edith Sitwell as well as scathing reviews of well-known writers. Young, affluent, and obviously talented, the poet thrived in literary Manhattan. He also cultivated friendships with Oscar Williams and Horace Gregory, two leading anthologists of the era.

America's entry into World War II brought Thompson's New York idyll to an end. Full of anxiety about his future, Thompson enlisted in 1942. His fears of an early death proved groundless. "I had a gallant war record," he remembered years later, "carrying Coca-Cola bottles to sergeants, and writing the Colonel's letters to friends back home. He used to mess up the grammar afterwards to make it sound authentic." In late 1943, Thompson was stationed in England. His light military duties allowed him to explore both London's literary world and its gay subculture. Despite the war, the gregarious Thompson moved with ease in literary circles meeting T. S. Eliot, Cyril Connolly, the Sitwells—finding, as Aiken observed, "all the Right People in two seconds flat." More important, in 1945 Thompson met Philip Trower, a young British intelligence officer on leave from Cairo. After being discharged from the Army later that year, he joined Trower in Cairo. They would spend the rest of their lives together.

The war did not stop Thompson's literary career. He published his first book, *Poems* (1943), in New York where it gathered considerable acclaim. An English edition followed three years later. Frail but delicately handsome, he was photographed in uniform by *Vogue*—the romantic embodiment of the aesthete soldier-poet. In 1946 Thompson's second book, *Lament for the Sleepwalkers*, appeared in the U.S. By then the author was in the Middle East researching a travel book, *The Phoenix in the Desert* (1951). By the time that he and Trower returned to England in 1947, Thompson had become a significant literary figure. Inspired by Thompson's example and success, Trower had also decided he would become a journalist.

Returning to England brought a serious complication. Thompson's legacy was not large enough to cover the costs of postwar London. As a temporary measure, he and Trower moved to the village of Cley next the Sea in Norfolk. Thompson probably assumed that his prose projects would soon allow them to return to the metropolis, but his travel book enjoyed only a modest success, and his novel, *The Dove with the Bough of Olives* (1954), proved a commercial failure. No more books would appear during his lifetime. Nor would he and Trower ever leave Cley.

In the meantime both men underwent a private transformation. Thompson had abandoned Catholicism at Harvard, though he had never entirely renounced the faith. In 1952 he told his lover (who had been raised an Anglican) that he wanted to practice the Catholic faith again. Trower was initially taken by surprise, but six months later he followed Thompson into the Church. The two men also made the bold move to ask for ecclesiastical permission to live together as a celibate couple, which, *mirabile dictu*, was granted. (Their spiritual advisor wisely felt that they would live their faith more successfully together than apart.) Although their platonic lifestyle has been criticized by some gay commentators (and their ecclesiastical license has astonished some Catholic ones), the couple's decision evidently worked. The two men spent the rest of their life together as a loving, contented, and very Catholic couple—a happiness attested to over the years by many visitors, both gay and straight. Thompson continued to write poetry but with little public success. A few poems appeared in the *New Yorker*, *Paris Review*, and *Horizon*, but his next three manuscripts remained unpublished in his lifetime. Meanwhile Trower prospered in his new career, eventually becoming a major Catholic journalist. Thompson died in 1975 after a long and painful decline from liver cancer. He was 57 years old. Trower continued as a journalist for the next forty years. Now 91, he lives in Cheltenham.

III

Beauty grows in you to the extent that love grows.
ST. AUGUSTINE

The young Thompson was a poet of evident power and individuality. His stylistic signature is so strong that one immediately recognizes his work, even in short quotations. The adjective habitually used to characterize his early verse is "baroque"—an evocative but inexact literary term, at least in English. In Romance language poetry, the baroque style emphasizes mood and rhetorical display over narrative description; it abounds in metaphorical conceits, complex puns, elaborate syntax, and unusual similes. Thompson, however, has little in common with baroque masters such as Luis de Góngora or Giambattista Marino—except in his Catholicism and penchant for elevated style. Presumably, critics have imported the term to suggest the emotional and stylistic extravagance of the early poems. Rather than the rhetorical and metaphorical bravado of a Góngora, in Thompson's case the term evokes the high drama of baroque painting and sculpture—replete with the martyred saints, yearning nudes, and shadowy revelers.

Significantly, the term "baroque" also carries a pejorative sense in English. Not surprisingly, it was first employed to censure Thompson in one of the earliest reviews of *Poems*. Howard Moss, later the poetry editor of the *New Yorker*, criticized the book's "baroque dishonesty," declaring that Thompson's poems "are moving, then, when they are most simple." Even when the poet's champions flourish the label approvingly, the term suggests that there is something at least potentially excessive and histrionic under discussion—a style that is richly fragrant but overly perfumed. The term will surely linger in Thompson's case and thereby continue to obscure the real source of the author's early style, the British New Romanticism of the 1940s. The precedent would have been obvious to the poet's early readers, but today it requires a scholarly gloss.

Despite his strong personality, the young Thompson wrote—with distinction and some originality—in a period style. Although one sees the American influences of Hart Crane and T. S. Eliot, his main influences were British—Gerard Manley Hopkins, Wilfred Owen, W. H. Auden, and Dylan Thomas. Thompson's key model, however, was George Barker, a leader of the neo-romantic revival. Now an author almost as obscure as Thompson, Barker, who was only five years older, already loomed as a major figure in the years just before World War II. A guilt-ridden, working-class ex-Catholic, Barker published his first book at twenty and became the youngest poet in W. B. Yeats's *Oxford Book of Modern Verse* (1936). His florid and fluent rhapsodies, rife with religious imagery and erotic reverie, proved immediately popular. With unintended prescience, Edwin Muir called him "a poet of genius at a still unformed stage." The tragedy of Barker's career was that his undeniably great talents never achieved meaningful formation. His work remained perpetually promising but persistently inchoate.

Most young poets borrow a style; few improve it. Thompson's accomplishment was to appropriate the elements of Barker's verse—the densely figurative language, pitched spiritual struggles, religious imagery, tortured eroticism, and self-dramatizing tone—and then employ them more powerfully than his master. Thompson takes the New Romantic style and pushes both the language and emotions further than Barker. In theory, this intensification of an already heated aesthetic would seem a dangerous strategy. In Thompson's idiosyncratic practice, it worked. Thompson created a poetic vehicle strong enough to carry his heavy anxieties—sexual, religious, political, and poetic. Here is the feverish and compelling "Tarquin," a portrait of a seductive sexual predator:

> The red-haired robber in the ravished bed
> Is doomsday driven, and averts his head,
> Turning to spurn the spoiled subjected body,
> That, lately lying altar for his ardor,
> Uncandled, scandalizes him, afraid he

Has lost his lifetime in a moment's murder:
He is the sinner who is saint instead:
The dark night makes him wish that he were dead.

What daring could not do, the drinks have done:
The limbo lad communicated one
Last sacrament, and, fast as falling, heaven
No longer held a stranger to emotion,
Who like a star, unsexed, unshamed, unshriven,
Was hurled, a lost world, whirling past damnation:
Circled by chaos but by eros spun,
The devil burned much brighter than the sun.

This bellboy beauty, this flamingo groom,
Who left his nickname soul too little room
For blood on blades of grass, must now turn over
Feel for the fatal flower, the hothouse sterile
Rose, raised in no god's praise, and, like death, never
Again enjoyed, must make his madness moral:
Washed by the inland waters of the womb,
The salt sheet is his shroud, the bed his tomb.

It is always difficult and sometimes fatal to measure the sincerity of a literary work. "All bad poetry," remarked Oscar Wilde, "springs from genuine feeling." Sincerity is no guarantee of artistic success, but at the heart of most literature is the urge to make the reader feel the reality of the writer's experience. In Thompson's case, the question of sincerity seems unavoidable. There are serious criticisms to be made of his early work—especially its prolixity, emotional self-absorption, and circumlocutionary structure. Why do these over-written and overheated lines nonetheless deliver such an emotional impact? What redeems the poem is its tangible sense of authen-ticity—*this is how it must actually feel*. This sincerity, in turn, seems to emerge from the confessional nature of the work.

The central impulse of Thompson's early poetry is lyric confession. The language is gorgeously decorated, the meter seductively steady, and the sins elaborately coded, but the confessional nature of the work is never ambiguous. The speaker compulsively bares his suffering and confusion to the reader—his hunger for male love, sexual guilt, painful romantic rejection, fear of death. Today these may be standard topics in undergraduate writing workshops, but in the wartime years these were not easy confessions to make, especially for an American in uniform. Thompson's self-exposure came at the risk of public shame and potential persecution—particularly the admission of homosexual affairs with fellow servicemen, which not only broke the law but also violated strict social codes of silence. "No tears in the writer," Robert Frost claimed, "no tears in the reader." Keening its vast and insistent threnody, the best of Thompson's tear-soaked early work transcends its own sentimentality mostly by its sheer frenetic persistence. All of the wrong notes seem small in comparison to its large, symphonic sweep.

The style of Thompson's early poetry is highly musical, metrically formal, and self-dramatizing. The language is packed with alliteration, internal rhyme, and assonance. The lines unfold sonorously in regular stanzas often mixing full and slant rhymes. There is lyrical repetition of lines and phrases. (The refrain is one of Thompson's signature devices.) The meter is almost always iambic, usually pentameter, a natural choice for a formal poet striving for resonant music. Thompson also occasionally employs iambic hexameter, which echoes the alexandrines of Charles Baudelaire and the Symbolists. Some poets underplay the metrical beat; Thompson accentuates it. One can recognize Thompson's hammered and alliterative style even in a single line:

> The red-haired robber in the ravished bed
> > "Tarquin"

> The head is human but the eyes are glass
> > "The Point of No Return"

> Narcissus, doubled in the melting mirror, smiles
> > "Largo"

Where is the clock to tell my time of tears
    "Where is the Clock to Tell My Time of Tears"

The strangler with his four and frantic hands
    "Lament for the Sleepwalker"

Thompson reveled in the hypnotic quality of formal rhythms. His mode is essentially rhapsodic—an attempt to cast an emotional spell over the listener. The structures of meaning are not logical or expository but musical. His poems move in circles with repeating words, lines, or refrains. His phrasing is often stylized and artificial, remote from the colloquial. Here is just half of the ornate and periphrastic opening sentence of "The Point of No Return":

See him now, how unhurried he destroys
The tick-tock meaning of the nursery boy's
Nostalgia for love's never-never land,
And, fairy-story prince turned toad, spews out.

Thompson's densely crafted poems communicate mostly through inference and association. (Here one sees the influence of Hart Crane, the master of lyric indirection.)

Thompson's aesthetic is auditory; the poems are meant to be heard. The rhetoric is overtly dramatic—usually spoken by an "I" often addressing a mysterious "You." "Water Music," which opens Thompson's first volume, *Poems*, begins:

Over the river, sleeping, sleep your nights
Of never my delights, of famous flights,
Not mine, outshining moonstone stars, displayed
Like summer sailors from black water drawn
To dance on malachite, to prance parade
Past queens last-quarter afternoons of dawn,
First sunset mornings, break-of-day midnights,
O as the snow swans end their Rhenish flights.

This passage is so flamboyantly overwritten that it acquires, amid its studied decadence, a sort of innocent and awkward charm. Ignoring the austerities of modern poetry, it unabashedly aspires towards the condition of music—the ripest late romantic music. Indeed, the author's intent is to *charm* in the older sense of creating an enchantment. Thompson casts a spell to bring the reader—and in a different way his lover—into a dark world that might otherwise seem forbidding. Seen from this perspective, Thompson's elaborate style is not simply a means to camouflage his homoerotic subject matter, it is also a musical formula to seduce the reader into feeling the private experiences being described.

"Water Music" presents its subject both directly (a nocturne sung to an absent lover) and indirectly (the images from the nocturnal world of rough trade along the docks). No degree in cryptography is required to decode the images of "summer sailors," "queens," and "swans." In Thompson's early books, the speaker is simultaneously intoxicated by the pleasures of casual sex and repelled by its predatory and reckless nature. No American poet had ever presented the homosexual milieu of the modern metropolis so frankly or so memorably. Auden had universalized the language of his love poems to mask their gay identity. Thompson's imagery is specifically homosexual. These are elegies on what Edward Field has called "pickups in the dark." Thompson's poems neither explicate nor document this underworld. Instead, they simply inhabit this secret city in vividly personal terms. In his combination of high romantic music, urban angst, and dark sexuality, the young Thompson found his distinctive voice.

IV

The punishment of every disordered mind is its own disorder.
ST. AUGUSTINE

The obsessive theme of Thompson's early work is the doomed relationship between sex and love in a perilous world. Even when he deals with other subjects, notably war and death, they are viewed through an erotic lens. Passionate, impulsive, and melancholy, these are the poems of a vulnerable young man, not sure of his place in the world and afraid of a war he cannot escape. The speaker's voice is so strongly defined—in both the best and worst poems—that a unified, autobiographical persona emerges whose erotic ardor and existential panic permeate both early volumes. The sexual vision is dark and dangerous. "The boy who brought me beauty brought me death," the speaker laments in "Articles of War"—one of the many lines in Thompson's work that prefigure the poetry of the AIDS era. Sexual beauty is accompanied by deception and menace, "For the devil, good-looking as a movie star, / Moves among us." Lost in a carnal wilderness in a treacherous time, the speaker longs for the certainty of a true, defining love. This repeated dream of a perfect and enduring union will prove to be what links Thompson's early poetry to his later work.

Thompson is a war poet of odd originality. He depicts World War II not as a battlefield or training ground—the usual settings of his soldier-poet contemporaries—but presents it indirectly through an urban nightscape of young men seeking furtive pleasure as they powerlessly await their destinies. The war is lethally real, but it remains elsewhere and invisible. The young soldier's anxiety is one of Thompson's recurring themes, but it usually serves as background for the erotic dramas unfolding in the poems. War sometimes serves simultaneously as subject and metaphor, as in one of Thompson's most compressed and accomplished poems, "This Loneliness for You Is Like the Wound":

88

This loneliness for you is like the wound
That keeps the soldier patient in his bed,
Smiling to soothe the general on his round
Of visits to the somehow not yet dead;
Who, after he has pinned a cross above
The bullet-bearing heart, when told that his
Is one who held the hill, bends down to give
Folly a diffident embarrassed kiss.
But once that medaled moment passes, O,
Disaster, charging on the fever chart,
Wins the last battle, takes the heights, and he
Succumbs before his reinforcements start.
Yet now, when death is not a metaphor,
Who dares to say that love is like the war?

This sonnet unfolds as a single extended simile, a metaphysical conceit that might actually be called baroque in the spirit of Giambattista Marino: the lover's loneliness is like a soldier's wound. Through synecdoche, the speaker then becomes the heroic, dying soldier who bears the wound. Reveling in the pathos of the situation, the speaker oddly resists its heroic implication. He presents the heroism ironically as a "folly" in a grotesque death scene with the general kissing the doomed man. The sonnet teeters on the edge of sentimentality and self-pity, but before the reader can bring this charge to the poem, the speaker delivers his own stern verdict in the self-lacerating final couplet, which dismisses the poetic fiction he has so carefully constructed. (The powerful use of the Shakespearean sonnet's closing couplet recalls a slightly earlier Shakespearean sonnet of the period, which also uses the war as a metaphor for personal anxiety—"For My Daughter" by Weldon Kees, a poet Thompson published in *Vice Versa*.)

The characteristic virtues of Thompson's early style—its extravagant music, feverish tone, coded eroticism, and circular structure—become its weaknesses when overextended. Composing his poems in formal stanzas, Thompson often tries to sustain his volatile and emotive tunes like a singer who repeats a refrain one time too many. The early poems are unabashedly ambitious—extended lyric odes in the romantic (and New Romantic) manner. The grandest of these odes is "Largo," the central work in *Poems*. Cast in an elaborate fifteen-line rhymed stanza of Thompson's own design, "Largo" stretches across 180 lines—longer than Keats's three greatest odes combined. Full of powerful feeling and lyric invention, this impressive exercise in the sublime is so fraught with literary allusion and histrionic gesture that it cannot carry the weight of its own aspirations. *Poems* also contains two other long sequences, "Articles of War" and "Images of Disaster," each of which runs eight pages, but neither poem summons even the intermittent power of "Largo." Thompson is at his best when most concentrated. Perhaps his finest early poem, "Tarquin," the chilling portrait of a ravishing predator, runs only three 8-line stanzas (in an intricate double-envelope rhyme scheme). It is surely significant that so many of Thompson's best poems, early and late, are sonnets. Fervor requires a framework.

V

What am I to you that you command me to love you?

ST. AUGUSTINE

Thompson returned to Catholicism in 1952. This decision, which reshaped his poetry, grew out of a new stability in his personal situation. The first half of his life had been largely itinerant; the second part settled securely in Norfolk. He had never before resided in the country. The quiet pace and solitude provided contemplative space that allowed him to reexamine his religious beliefs. Thompson's literary success had never been commercial, but he had enjoyed considerable recognition since his early twenties. As his public career faded after the failure of his novel, Cley also protected him from both the cultural competition and financial pressures of London. Norfolk's isolation allowed him to moderate the heavy social drinking that had characterized his New York and London years. His inner life calmed. His turbulent search for "the always loving heart" had led him to Trower, his spiritual hungers back to his childhood faith. "I'm so grateful to God for keeping me hidden away in this unknown village," he remarked shortly before his death. Not surprisingly, these profound changes transformed his poetry, though not exactly in the ways some critics have maintained.

A common assumption about Thompson's career is that he changed from a glorious gay pagan celebrating the world, the flesh, and the devil to a pious Catholic contemplating eternity, the soul, and salvation. Such a neat dichotomy makes it easy to generalize about the poetry. The problem is that a careful study of the work itself does not support the theory that Thompson changed (in Edward Field's pithy but inaccurate formula) "from brilliant bad boy to repentant sinner." The poems tell a more complicated and interesting story. They demonstrate both continuities and dislocations in his work. They also suggest that Thompson's main transformation was not theological but emotional.

There is no confusing Thompson's early and later verse. They not only differ in style; the tone, manner, and subjects of the two periods also bear little resemblance to one another. If Thompson's early verse is flamboyantly neo-romantic, the later work is calmly neo-classical. It eschews emotional fervor for measured reflection. No longer agonizingly searching for his place in the world, the poet speaks from the security of a meaningfully situated life. A reader may disagree with Thompson's choices—some proponents of the early work have—but there is no disputing the psychological and emotional stability that characterizes the later poems. "I owe my heart / Unfettered and my soul at rest. / To you, who offer more than all my art / Can match," he writes in a late poem to Trower. A critic may miss the youthful *Sturm und Drang*; Thompson did not. "Only the old are grateful," he writes, "not the young."

Freed from the traumatic struggles that had previously formed its central subject, Thompson's poetry either had to change or sink into self-parody. His solution was to reinvent himself—from a Dionysian romantic with a single lyric style and subject into an Apollonian classicist exploring a great variety of subjects, forms, and genres. His style cooled becoming more austere and controlled. The tone shifted from vatic to conversational. The growth of his verse technique is also noteworthy. If Thompson's early work is characterized by its masterful use of iambic pentameter, the later poetry displays metrical diversity and formal experimentation. His prosodic patterns change from page to page. For the first time he uses free verse. No longer locked into a single rhapsodic mode, Thompson writes dramatic monologues, narratives, hymns, satires, epigrams, epistles, devotions, discursive meditations, as well as short lyrics. Thompson also became prolific. The "Red Book," as the posthumously published *Poems: 1950-1974* is often called, contains five times as many poems as the two early books combined. It is not surprising that readers smitten by the early poems find the later work foreign. It changed radically in most respects. What unites Thompson's earlier and later work is his personal identity as both gay and Catholic. The expression of that complicated double identity differs significantly, but it persists as an animating presence. The obvious fact that some of Thompson's gay advocates and Catholic admirers find the combination troublesome does not alter its continuity.

It is a great mistake to divide Thompson's career into Catholic and non-Catholic periods. Roman Catholicism haunts all of his writing, even the novel and travelogue. The early poetry is as deeply and explicitly theological as the later work. What mostly differs is the speaker's perceived relationship toward grace and redemption. Edward Field's formula is exactly backwards: only in Thompson's early work does the persona of the guilt-ridden sinner appear. This torturously divided soul, vacillating between carnal desire and spiritual despair, serves as the protagonist of the early work. If the young Thompson was indeed a "brilliant bad boy," he was also the very poster child of Catholic guilt. For him, sexual inebriation inevitably led to a theological hangover. By contrast, the calm and grateful persona of the later work is unconcerned with guilt or repentance.

The title of the early poem "Memorare," for instance, which means "remember" in Latin, alludes to a popular Catholic prayer of "guilty and sorrowful" supplication to the Virgin Mary. On a literal level, "Memorare" is a war poem in the form of a benediction for the "lost lads" killed in battle on earth, air, and sea. Oddly for an American poem written in the aftermath of the Battle of Britain and London Blitz, Thompson's lament mourns all the dead, allied or enemy, who share physical destruction, erotic desolation, and spiritual abandonment. Published a month before Pearl Harbor, the poem's neutrality was not yet politically problematic, but this verse prayer remains the strangest war poem of the period—simultaneously a religious lament and homoerotic elegy for the young male dead. The dead lads in uniform are so explicitly eroticized as lovers, often in homosexual terms—"a gay ghost at land's end," for instance—that it is difficult not to feel "Memorare" as a universal gay lament. It is unclear who the "you" addressed in the poem is—God, the Virgin Mary, all enlisted men, humanity itself, or just the poet—though its devotional rhetoric suggests a supernatural agency. Whomever it invokes, "Memorare" never ceases to be a prayer of both curtailed love and sorrowful supplication. It concludes:

> Remember the enemy, always remembering you,
> Whose heartbreaks heartbeat defeats, who too,
> Shedding tears during prayers for the dead, discovers
> Himself forever alone, the last of his lovers
> Laid low for love, and, O at your mercy, murdered.
> *The lost lads are gone*
> *God grace them*

To miss the Catholicism in Thompson's early work is to misread it. Although the early lyrics deal obsessively with love and sex, the context in which the poet presents his erotic struggle is theological and specifically Catholic. Here is a stanza from one of Thompson's most explicitly sexual poems, "The Point of No Return," a nightmare vision of a gay Times Square hustler and drug addict:

> What welter of the womb that air breath day
> The serpent signified once more in clay:
> Later, the data of a Christ-crossed class
> The garbage gift of faith, slag heap of hope,
> Concerning charity—the sounding brass:
> Those cardinals triple crowned this antipope,
> Whose keys are skeleton, whose ring is gay
> With fools for jewels, whose blessings playboys pray.

In eight lines, one finds twelve Catholic images and allusions: the serpent, Christ, the cross, the three theological virtues of faith, hope, and charity, cardinals, the papal crown, the antipope, ring, keys, and a phrase from St. Paul's First Epistle to the Corinthians. (One could press four further claims—womb, clay, blessings, and pray—but the point is already made.) Why is there such an extraordinary density of sacred imagery in a poem ostensibly about a street hustler? Thompson's feverish dramas exist in a theological framework. The sordid and sexual are inseparable from the supernatural.

There has been a hesitation among both gay and Christian readers to recognize that Thompson's homosexuality and Catholicism co-exist throughout his career. Just as the early poems are saturated with religion, the later work continues to reflect his gay identity—not perhaps in ways consistent with current orthodox opinion but nonetheless apparent. Sexuality has many expressions, including celibacy. Thompson's return to Catholic practice did not change his sexual orientation or eradicate his libido; it only provided the spiritual means to sublimate eros into agape. (Trower's unpublished memoir makes it clear that neither man denied his sexual orientation, however much they controlled its physical expression.) The "Red Book" contains several love poems to Trower, which may be chaste but are nonetheless full of passionate devotion to the man Thompson felt had redeemed his life.

There is also a common notion that Catholic poetry is a literature of saintly and well-behaved writers—a pious cliché shared by some Catholic and secular critics. This platitude has no basis in either theology or literary history. There is, of course, a great tradition of Catholic devotional literature from Boethius and Hildegard von Bingen to Thomas Merton and Simone Weil. Most Catholic imaginative literature, however, has been obsessed with sin. To be a Catholic is to recognize one's self as a sinner in a fallen world, and the central narrative of Catholic literature is the sinner's difficult journey toward salvation. Dante's *Commedia*, which begins in the dark wood of the author's own depravity, presents the full journey of the spirit from perdition to redemption. Many great writers, however, have portrayed only the darker part of the journey—often because that is where their own lives have stalled. Take, for instance, two authors whom Thompson greatly admired, François Villon and Charles Baudelaire. They were both self-proclaimed sinners, who declared they were likely destined for damnation. Baudelaire and Villon were no less Catholic for their sinfulness. Like salvation, damnation has its literary canon. Catholicism is a faith and world-view, not an outcome. From this perspective, Thompson's early poetry, which portrays his tormented struggle toward redemption, is both a landmark in American gay literature and his greatest contribution to modern Catholic literature.

Ironically, Catholicism is actually less visible in Thompson's later work. He does not disguise his faith, but he doesn't so habitually present it. *Poems: 1950-1974* contains some devotional poems, but religion is not its primary topic. The central subject is quite secular, namely history. The older Thompson obsessively ponders the past as a window into the human condition. His interests range from India and China to the United States and Panama, but his main focus is Europe, especially its ancient history. Thompson meditates on the lives of emperors, tyrants, philosophers, poets, and soldiers.

He imagines "Ovid on the Dacian Coast," "Hannibal at the Armenian Court," and "Virgil at Brundisium." There are over a hundred historical poems in the posthumous collection. Thompson's subject matter is notably similar to that of another gay Christian poet fascinated by history, Constantine Cavafy, a lax and lubricious yet loyal Greek Orthodox. Thompson writes poems on historical Christian subjects, such as his epigrammatic sequence on St. Augustine and his passionate sonnet on Cardinal Manning, the great Victorian champion of social justice for the poor. But usually Thompson, like Cavafy, finds sinners more interesting than saints. Of course, there is a case to be made that Thompson's choice of history as his subject betrays his essentially Catholic imagination, which takes as its natural purview the long perspective from the present back to the time of Christ and the Caesars.

The mature Thompson also reveals a surprising gift for epigram, a linguistic compression impossible to predict from his expansive early work. The "Red Book" is full of epigrammatic verse, some self-contained, some remarkably built into sequences. Appropriating the classical tradition of Martial and the Greek Anthology, Thompson uses the form to ponder eminent figures of antiquity in superbly pointed epigrams on Seneca, Tacitus, Apollodorus of Athens, Caligula, Nero, and many others. In "Horace," Thompson neatly anatomizes the great Latin poet in a way that touches on the tensions and temptations of his own literary career:

> Perfection measured into every part:
> Nothing is wanting save, perhaps a heart;
> But when you are so clever from the start,
> Love almost always loses out to art.

VI

Take up and read.
ST. AUGUSTINE

There is a final factor to consider in Thompson's later development. In middle age a writer gains perspective on his own life and work. He also better understands the careers of his contemporaries. Thompson's early adulthood was characterized by passionate excess. Both his poetry and literary identity emerged from that intense but precarious existence, an unstable mix creativity and anxiety, love and promiscuity, exuberant sociability and alcoholism. As the fuel that fired his poetry, Thompson's life risked becoming aestheticized into a self-consuming artifact. Settled in Norfolk, he pondered the lethal toll that alcoholic disorder and emotional exhibitionism had taken on his contemporaries. "Some I knew / Took to drink / And died gladly," Thompson writes in "Memoirs," observing how many of his contemporaries were destroyed by sex or alcohol. "There were writers / Who did not write / Or wrote badly." Dylan Thomas had died at 39. George Barker had sunk into self-parody. (Hart Crane's alcoholic decline and early suicide haunted Thompson, eventually becoming the subject of one of his last, longest, and worst poems.) The failure of New Romanticism was not only aesthetic but moral; it fostered a voyeuristic cult of the self-destructive artist pushing experience to the limit for the delectation of the audience. A quarter century later the pathological tendency would reemerge as Confessional poetry and contribute to the deaths of John Berryman, Anne Sexton, and others. Thompson must have felt that he had pushed that style of both life and poetry far enough. To survive meant to change.

If critics have not yet done full justice to Thompson's early work, the later poetry remains mostly unstudied and unknown. Anyone evaluating it faces three major obstacles—its abundance, diversity, and varying quality. There are 259 poems in the posthumous

97

volume, many of them long. By comparison there were only 45 poems in the two early collections. The late poems also divide into many different forms and genres, some of which seem more natural to Thompson's talents than others. All of Thompson's work is uneven. The second half of *Poems* (1943), for instance, is markedly inferior to the first half. *Poems: 1950-1974* is full of weak or minor poems. Thompson's penchant for travel poems, in particular, resulted in a kind of elegant verse journalism. The "Red Book" contains dozens of colorful but not especially memorable views of foreign cities and landscapes. The travel poems are perceptive and intelligent but lack emotional force and personal connection. Likewise some of the religious poetry is diffuse, prosaic, or senti-mental. As in the early work, compression focuses Thompson's gifts; the best devotional poems are mostly short. But the "Red Book" also reveals poetic growth. The title of one of the best late poems, "Introspection," characterizes one particularly compelling change. Here the aging poet ponders his own romantic origins with empathy and insight: "My eye aches—the eye / Is a mirror where / Self-deceptions try / Vainly to disappear." In poems such as "Introspection," "Youth," "In Rain, in Loneliness, the Late Despair," thought is animated by powerful emotion. The two Dunstan Thompsons, for a moment at least, become one.

Dunstan Thompson is not a major poet, but he is also not a minor writer in the conventional sense of doing a few things exquisitely well. He is ambitious, original, mercurial, and uneven in equal measures. His central themes—love, sex, desire, faith, war, and history—are not minor subjects. When he fails, which is often, it is not from timidity but because he reaches for something beyond his capacity to convey. He wrote too much and often too obsessively about the same subjects. Reading him, one must overlook the flaws to find the virtues. Thompson did not change American poetry. He burned brightly for a few years, and then disappeared from public view. He left no direct literary heirs, but he has sustained a following for half a century. His voice remains vital and genuinely expressive. Thompson occupies a unique place in both Catholic and gay American letters, as well as in the literature of World War II. He will never be a popular poet, but there will be readers drawn to the passions he explores. They will not find his like elsewhere.

Brother Beat Meets Mr. Everson

Seventy years ago, Catholicism decisively entered the mainstream of American literature. A formidable group of writers, including Flannery O'Connor, Katherine Anne Porter, J. F. Powers, Thomas Merton, Robert Lowell, and Allen Tate became the first generation of American Catholics to gain major reputations. Theological ideas pervaded cultural discourse, not only from Catholic intellectuals such as Jacques Maritain, Wallace Fowlie, and Marshall McLuhan but from non-believers such as Alfred Kazin and Leslie Fiedler. Literary conversions—Ernest Hemingway, Tennessee Williams, Countee Cullen—became newsworthy events. It was not only acceptable for a writer to be a practicing Catholic; back then, it actually seemed chic.

In that diverse creative cohort, no figure was more interesting than the Beat poet William Everson, who at the height of the San Francisco Renaissance briefly achieved celebrity as Brother Antoninus. Although his critical reputation has declined since his death in 1994, Everson remains a writer of substantial achievement as well as a major figure in the history of fine press printing. His odd and often torturous life also illustrates the spiritual strengths and perils of the Catholic convert.

William Oliver Everson was born in Sacramento, California, in 1912, the second of three children to a mismatched couple. The poet's father, a Norwegian immigrant, had come to America alone as a boy. His wife, who was fifteen years younger, grew more emotionally distant from her husband with the birth of each child. "In the world of the myth," the poet later commented, "my mother was a goddess and my father was an ogre." The young Everson received little religious training. His Catholic mother had converted to Christian Science before drifting into religious indifference. In 1914, his family moved to Selma, a small farming town in the San Joaquin Valley where his father worked as a bandmaster. A poor student, Everson graduated from Selma Union High School in 1931. He entered Fresno State College but quickly dropped out. Enlisting in the Civilian Conservation Corps, a Roosevelt administration jobs program, he spent the next year building roads and trails in Sequoia National Park. This early stint established a pattern of physical labor, close connection to nature, and solitary contemplation that continued through the poet's life.

Returning to Fresno State in 1934, Everson made the crucial literary discovery of his life—the poetry of Robinson Jeffers. It was nothing short of a conversion. "Suddenly the whole inner world began to tremble," he later described his first reading of Jeffers's work. Everson's lifelong devotion to Jeffers rivals in depth and intensity any case of poetic emulation on record—comparable to Charles Baudelaire's obsession with Edgar Allan Poe. Everson's affinity with Jeffers went beyond mere literary influence. It reflected deep imaginative and moral connections. Jeffers taught him to see the California landscape and through it to recognize the natural world as primal reality.

Everson's long study and profound identification with the older poet led to two probing and impassioned critical studies, *Robinson Jeffers: Fragments of an Older Fury* (1968) and *The Excesses of God: Robinson Jeffers as a Religious Figure* (1988). More important, his encounter with Jeffers confirmed the young man's literary vocation. "I began to write other poems," he recalled, "and by the end of the semester I knew what I was going to do." Once again dropping out of college, Everson embarked on a life of poetry. Supporting himself as an irrigation pipe layer and cannery worker, he published his first two volumes, *These Are the Ravens* (1935) and *San Joaquin* (1939), with small California presses. Meanwhile he married his high school girlfriend and bought a small farm.

Rooted in the agricultural landscape of central California, Everson's early poems are compressed, lyrical, and imagistic. He had not yet discovered Catholicism, but these youthful works are already suffused with a genuine, if still vague, religious longing. Take, for instance, "These Are the Ravens," in which the central image is both California's common raven and the prophetic fowls of the Old Testament:

> These are the ravens of my soul,
> Sloping above the lonely fields
> And cawing, cawing.
> I have released them now,
> And sent them wavering down the sky,
> Learning the slow witchery of the wind,
> And crying on the farthest fences of the world.

In 1940 American men were required to register for possible military conscription. Europe was already at war. Everson filed as a conscientious objector. When the United States declared war on the Axis powers, the 30-year-old Everson was called up and sent to Civilian Public Service Camp 56 in Waldport, Oregon, where he worked with other COs clearing trails and crushing rocks. The camp contained a small bohemia of intellectuals, writers, actors, and artists, including George Woodcock, Adrian Wilson, and Clayton James. Internees produced plays, held debates, and even opened an art school. Under the liberal supervision of a Camp Director, who was himself a CO, wartime discipline was relaxed. Walport published both an official newsletter, *Tide*, and an underground anarchist journal, *Untide*. Everson not only contributed to the illicit newsletter but also helped print it—his introduction to letterpress work, the craft he would eventually master. He corresponded with radical writers such as Henry Miller and Kenneth Rexroth. He set up a small literary press. Ironically, the confinement camp became Everson's university.

The poet's personal life changed dramatically during this three-year incarceration. His father died. (His mother had passed away in 1940.) His wife left him for another man. After being demobilized in 1946, a dispirited Everson returned to California to set up a letterpress in a Sonoma County commune. Quickly falling in love, he moved to Berkeley to court an artist who was in the process of rediscovering her Catholic faith. She was not to be seduced, but she gave him a copy of St. Augustine's *Confessions*, thereby introducing him to the other decisive author in his life.

At a midnight Mass on Christmas Eve, 1948, Everson underwent a mystical experience. The following July he was baptized at St. Augustine's Church in Oakland. He soon began working for Dorothy Day's Catholic Worker movement on Oakland's Skid Row, which provided food and lodging for the homeless. In his private devotions Everson continued to have ecstatic mystical encounters. "I was seized with a feeling so intense as to exceed anything I had previously experienced," he recorded in a notebook. "It was a feeling of extreme anguish and joy, of transcendent spirituality and of great, thrilling physical character. . . . From the tabernacle had issued to me something like an intense invisible ray, a dark ray, like a ray of light seen in the mind only."

In 1951 Everson joined the Dominican order as a lay brother (a member of the community with no intention of becoming a priest and, therefore, under no immediate obligation to take binding vows of poverty, obedience, and chastity). Given the name Antoninus, the poet entered St. Albert's College, a monastery in Oakland. In addition to washing dishes and cleaning the sacristy, the new brother set up his letterpress in the basement. Soon he started working on an elaborate folio edition of the Latin Psalter recently authorized by Pius XII, a book which would eventually be recognized as a master-piece of American hand-press printing.

Everson's conversion unleashed a torrent of poetic creation. Many critics consider the three collections he published as Brother Antoninus his finest poetic works — *The Crooked Lines of God* (1959), *The Hazards of Holiness* (1962), and *The Rose of Solitude* (1967), which were later collected in *The Veritable Years: 1949-1966* (1978). In this feverishly visionary poetry, Everson abandoned his austere earlier style to create a larger lyrical mode. The poems expand to contain the ebb and tide of the author's exhilaration, ecstasy, and despair.

As poet William Stafford observed, this work offers "a shock and a delight to break free into the heart's unmanaged impulses."

As Brother Antoninus, Everson became one of the key figures of the San Francisco Renaissance—the "Beat Friar" featured in *Time* magazine dressed in Dominican robes dramatically intoning his work to huge audiences. What does Catholic Beat poetry sound like? Here are a few lines from "The Making of the Cross," a rhapsodic ode that imagines how the wood and iron that crucified Jesus came to be at Golgotha:

> Just as in life the good things of the earth
> Are patiently assembled: some from here, some from there;
> Wine from the hill and wheat from the valley;
> Rain that comes blue-bellied out of the sopping sea;
> Snow that keeps its drift on the gooseberry ridge,
> Will melt with May, go down, take the egg of the salmon,
> Serve the traffic of otters and fishes,
> Be ditched to orchard. . . .
>
> So too are gathered up the possibles of evil.

Fame proved Brother Antoninus's undoing. Although Everson wanted to deepen his religious commitment, his public life provided too many temptations. Soon after taking his initial three-year vow to join the First Order, he became involved with a young woman who had come to him for counseling. In 1969 Everson left the Dominicans to marry her. With typical panache, he publicly announced his new life by stripping off his clerical robes at the end of a poetry reading and then leaving the hall. Brother Antoninus was no more.

The newly secularized Everson took a position as the poet-in-residence of Kresge College at the University of California at Santa Cruz. He also founded Lime Kiln Press to continue printing. He composed poetry prolifically, publishing three substantial collections in close succession, *Man-Fate* (1974), *River Root* (1976), and

The Masks of Drought (1980). At Lime Kiln he produced a series of celebrated limited editions, most notably *Granite & Cypress* (1975), a hand-printed selection of Jeffers's poems, set in a cypress box with a polished granite centerpiece. (A copy now sells for about twenty thousand dollars.) In 1977 Everson was at the height of his fame when he developed Parkinson's disease. Five years later the illness forced him to close his press. He retreated to Kingfisher Flat, his cabin in the hills above Santa Cruz. After a long and painful decline, he died in 1994.

Everson's most important later work was his critical prose. At Santa Cruz, he taught a popular year-long course on the poetic vocation. At that time Santa Cruz was the University of California's experimental campus. It recruited progressive faculty, such as Norman O. Brown, George Hitchcock, and Gregory Bateson, with the aim of transforming undergraduate education. Letter grades were eliminated. Everson's course had no homework, papers, or exams. Twice a week students would gather in a geodesic dome to sit on pillows and listen to his charismatic lectures. Influenced by Karl Jung's theories of myth and archetype, Everson strived to integrate his compendious literary and theological sources to understand the process of poetic creation. He was particularly interested in the connection between the imagination and the natural landscape. This relationship, he hypothesized, was the crucial fact in West Coast consciousness. "When you get to the Pacific," he wrote, "there is really no further place to go. . . . there is a sense of termination." Old notions of America no longer suffice. "It is a mystery, and it is a threat; the soul is revulsed to find itself at the end of the line."

Everson's critical methods seem unconventional when compared with the academic scholarship of his contemporaries. He does not proceed by careful citation, systematic analysis, and linear argumentation. His approach is subjective, panoramic, and associative, though also deeply learned. His methods, however, were firmly based in Catholic contemplative literature. "Suffice it to say," Everson explained, "that when I left the monastery for academe the method that I brought with me was meditative rather than discursive. For I had learned how concepts seemingly exhausted by endless repetition could suddenly, under the probe of intuition, blossom into life."

In his late critical works, Everson analyzed the artistic and spiritual forces that had created the distinctive cultural vision of California and the far West. He began by chronicling its literary history in *Archetypes West: The Pacific Coast as a Literary Region* (1976). Historian Kevin Starr aptly described the volume as "a plateau in California's continual quest for self-knowledge and symbolic self-awareness." Everson never synthesized his diverse materials, which included theology, anthropology, literature, history, and geology, into a single system, but slowly he developed a range of perspectives on American regional ecosystems and their impact on human creativity. Everson published the results of his studies as a series of interlocking essays in *Birth of a Poet: The Santa Cruz Meditations* (1982). This magisterial volume remains one of the best books ever written about Western literature. His late prose is sometimes prophetic in tone, but the style is lucid, concise, and colloquial. *Birth of a Poet* is written entirely in short mediations linked in thematic chains. Here is one typically brief section:

> The unconscious religion in the West is pantheism. Nature seems to carry the whole thrust of the divine. Established religions have a very shallow footing in the West. It is as if the California experience of religion is affective, something entering into you in a physical way. Especially in the coastal region, where there is the great drop-off point and the intensity of the sea, sustained church-going is difficult. Why should we sit in church on a Sunday when God is walking on water out there?

Encyclopedic, idiosyncratic, and yet compellingly readable, *Birth of a Poet* defies summary. Like Ezra Pound's *ABC of Reading* or D. H. Lawrence's *Studies in Classical American Literature*, the book radiates the mysterious energy of personal necessity—an absolutely committed writer trying to get at the hidden center of his art. *Birth of a Poet* represents the capstone to Everson's polymathic career. It is a work of rewarding originality and passionate engagement with the world. It says a great deal about the marginality of Western writing that this still urgently relevant volume is not better known.

Whether he worked in poetry, prose, or typography, Everson vividly embodied the tradition of the prophetic visionary. His artistic legacy remains unique—with enduring achievements in three fields. He left a small but individual body of religious poetry in which the natural world is suffused with the divine. He published hand-printed editions that rank among the high points of American book arts. He wrote some of the most ambitious critical studies of California literature and its complex relations to American letters, books of such intellectual intensity and strong style that they seem perpetually new. No critic has more profoundly articulated what it means to be a West Coast author. In these varied accomplishments, Everson represents a fascinating part of the American Catholic literary tradition—a legacy still too little known, even by Catholics.

Clarify Me, Please, God of the Galaxies: Elizabeth Jennings

The English poet Elizabeth Jennings had the peculiar fate of being in the right place at the right time in the wrong way. Her career began splendidly. Her verse appeared in prominent journals, championed by Oxford's new generation of tastemakers. Her first publication, *Poems* (1952), launched the acclaimed Fantasy Poets pamphlet series, which would soon present early work by Philip Larkin, Kingsley Amis, Thom Gunn, and Geoffrey Hill. Her first full-length collection, *A Way of Looking* (1955), won the Somerset Maugham Award and became the Poetry Book Society recommendation. She was the youngest poet featured in the first *Penguin Modern Poets* volume (1962). Meanwhile Jennings achieved enduring notoriety as the only female member of "The Movement," the irreverent and contrarian group who dominated mid-century British poetry. By age thirty, Jennings was a celebrated writer.

"To be lucky in the beginning is everything," claimed Cervantes, but Jennings's luck did not hold. In the great expansion of universities and literary publishing following World War II, her Movement peers gained academic appointments, lucrative book deals, and critical esteem. Jennings's career stalled. Her fame as a Movement poet proved a dead end. She never belonged in that Oxbridge boys club. She shared the Movement's commitment to clarity and traditional form, but her politics were to the left of their mostly conservative stance. Deeper than politics, however, were two fundamental differences between Jennings and her peers. "I was a woman and also a Roman Catholic," she later observed, "which meant that I wanted to write about subjects which were simply uninteresting to most Movement poets." Her emotionally direct verse, which pondered love, art, and religion, had little in common with their detached and ironic attitude toward experience.

There were also personal impediments to her continued success. Physically and emotionally frail, Jennings was not able to sustain a practical career. She lacked the temperament for any employment but poetry. She drifted between failed jobs and impossible lovers. She was hospitalized for mental illness. By forty, she had sunk into poverty, rescued only by the occasional publisher's advance or literary prize. Alone and destitute in old age, Jennings moved from one short-term lodging to another, a shabby eccentric haunting Oxford cafés.

The sorrows of poets are legion and their failures commonplace. Why does the case of Elizabeth Jennings deserve special consideration? Despite her worldly failures, her artistic career was a steady course of achievement. Jennings ranks among the finest British poets of the second half of the twentieth century. She is also England's best Catholic poet since Gerard Manley Hopkins.

Jennings was a writer of prodigious productivity. She published twenty-seven collections of verse and half a dozen critical volumes. Her reputation would be larger had she published less. Few scholars have come to terms with the intimidating scale of her oeuvre. Her posthumous *Collected Poems* (2012), edited by Emma Mason, contains more than 1,300 poems, and it did not reprint everything. "I write fast and revise very little," Jennings declared. Her huge corpus is uneven. How could it not be? The early work is stronger and more consistent, but she wrote superb poems at every stage of her career, if one has the stamina to find them. (There is an urgent need for a new selected volume of her verse.)

Jennings always had a few champions among fellow poets. Anne Stevenson claimed that Jennings had written "some of the finest lyric poetry of the twentieth century." Anthony Thwaite once ranked her and Larkin as his two favorite poets of the Movement. In the small society of British letters, however, Jennings's personal decline eroded her critical reputation. As Martin Booth observed, Jennings was "great as a poet, but she doesn't look it." When she accepted a CBE from the Queen in 1992, the impoverished poet wore a knitted hat, duffle coat, and canvas shoes. The tabloids dubbed Jennings "the bag-lady of the sonnets." The epithet stuck.

Although mocked by the press and neglected by scholars, Jennings enjoyed a popular readership in the U.K. Her *Selected Poems* (1979) sold 50,000 copies. Her poems became A-level texts for secondary schools. Her steadfast publisher, Michael Schmidt of Carcanet, claims she became his best-selling author—"the most unconditionally loved" poet of her generation. In the U.S., however, Jennings remains unknown, even among Christian literati whose knowledge of British Catholic verse often ends with G. K. Chesterton.

Jennings was born in Boston, Lincolnshire, in 1926, the younger daughter of a doctor, who served as County Medical Officer. When she was six, the family moved to Oxford, where the poet would remain for nearly all of the next seventy years. The Tolkien family members were fellow parishioners, and their daughter Priscilla became Elizabeth's lifelong friend. Jennings attended a Catholic primary school and then entered Oxford High School. Her teenage years were lonely and unhappy, "a very, very dark period," she later recalled. From 1944 to 1947 she studied English at St. Anne's College, the first women's college at Oxford. These were happier times as Jennings pursued poetry and boys pursued her. She attended C. S. Lewis's lectures and acted in the Experimental Theatre Club. Her literary talent was recognized by other Oxford poets, such as Larkin and Amis, whom critics would soon group with her in The Movement. After graduation, she followed an older man, who had been a Japanese Prisoner of War, to London, where she worked as a copywriter. Both the job and her engagement soon ended. The disappointed Jennings returned to Oxford, where she found a position at the city library. Neither jobs nor love affairs— all unconsummated, though not all platonic—would prove lasting.

In 1957, however, the Maugham prize required Jennings to spend three months abroad. She chose Rome. Her time in Italy not only inspired some of her most radiant poetry. It also revitalized her

Catholic faith. Her early religious upbringing had left her tormented with guilt. Now in the historical center of Catholicism, she experienced her faith as a joyful presence in the churches and art. "I really found happiness," she recalled forty years later in a BBC interview. Rome also enlarged her artistic vision—supplementing her vivid sensory imagination with a metaphysical dimension. Her next collection, *A Sense of the World* (1958), contained a section of devotional poems animated by what critic Margaret Willy termed the struggle to find "the elusive language capable of expressing the numinous."

Back in England, however, Jennings's life slowly fell apart. For two years she worked unhappily as a publisher's reader for Chatto and Windus, spending part of each week in London. The strain led to a physical and emotional collapse. Jennings resolved to make her living as a freelance writer. Money troubles soon followed. She drank heavily. Her elderly parents moved from Oxford. Another romantic relationship ended. Jennings made a series of suicide attempts. In 1962 she was sent to Guy's Hospital in London. Calmed with drugs, she was placed in psychotherapy, a process that she found painful and unproductive. She was also shocked by the suffering of her fellow patients, whose private infirmities were not easily cured in that era of electroconvulsive therapy, Freudian analysis, and heavy medication.

Jennings's experiences with mental breakdown and hospitalization parallel those of several of her American "Confessional School" contemporaries—Robert Lowell, Anne Sexton, John Berryman, and Sylvia Plath. As in their work, collapse, confinement, and rehabilitation became subjects for poetry. Her next collections, *Recoveries* (1964) and *The Mind Has Mountains* (1966), contain powerful accounts of mental illness, most notably her "Sequence in Hospital," which chronicles her time at St. Guy's. It was characteristic that her poems attended to the plight of other patients as much as her own dire predicament.

The woman who emerged from St. Guy's was a vulnerable and chastened person. Her youth was over, and her resources drained. She would never marry nor enjoy a reliable source of income. Her life would be plagued by recurring penury, loneliness, alcoholism, and depression. For the next four decades she survived on the margins of Oxford, helpless to reverse her fortunes—"Orphaned and elderly and yet a child." Her creative energy, however, remained undiminished. Jennings published two dozen more collections of verse. The agony and humiliation of her breakdown also changed her work. Not only did her language and meter relax, her perspective shifted. As an unsigned obituary in the *Telegraph* observed, she developed "from an essentially thinking poet to a poet of feeling and suffering."

There are two ways to introduce an unfamiliar poet. The first and less effective way is to describe the particular qualities of the work. Critics have struggled to characterize what makes Jennings's work so attractive. The words most often used are "introspective," "formal," "reticent," and "clear." Those adjectives are not inaccurate, but they miss her poetry's compelling intimacy and delicate beauty. Thwaite comes closer by pairing the work's contradictory qualities. Jennings's poetry, he proposed, is "rational but open to mystery, tender but unsentimental, expressed in words that were almost always pure, clear, gravely lyrical and committed to a sense of hard-won order out of chaos."

The second way to introduce a poet is simpler. Quote the work. Here is the opening of "I Feel."

> I feel I could be turned to ice
> If this goes on, if this goes on.
> I feel I could be buried twice
> And still the death not yet be done.
>
> I feel I could be turned to fire
> If there can be no end to this.
> I know within me such desire
> No kiss could satisfy, no kiss.

The poem's language is direct, musical, and intense. The strict form feels less like an abstract framework than a cauldron barely able to contain its scalding emotions. The poem's impact is so immediate and tangibly personal that it is easy to miss its quiet but profound engagement with the Catholic literary tradition. The paradoxical combination of ice and fire imagery goes back at least as far as Petrarch. More interesting, however, is the poem's connections to Christian mysticism. Although "I Feel" initially seems an expression of erotic longing poisoned by despair, close examination reveals it can also be read as a tortured expression of spiritual hunger, the mystic's excruciating desire for rapturous union with God.

Christianity was not a secondary concern to Jennings. Asked for a personal statement about her work by *Contemporary Poets*, she replied, "My Roman Catholic religion and my poems are the most important things in my life." Much of her work is explicitly religious. Among her best poems are vivid representations of Gospel episodes—"The Annunciation," "The Visitation," and "Lazarus." These devotional poems are neither pious nor abstract. Jennings places herself directly in each scene as an observer—in a manner similar to Ignatian meditation—and experiences the mysteries in human terms. In "The Resurrection" Jennings imagines herself a doubting Thomas at the empty grave. Written in her signature form, rhymed quatrains, it begins:

> I was the one who waited in the garden
> Doubting the morning and the early light.
> I watched the mist lift off its own soft burden,
> Permitting not believing my own sight.
>
> If there were sudden noises I dismissed
> Them as a trick of sound, a sleight of hand.
> Not by a natural joy could I be blessed
> Or trust a thing I could not understand.

In her absorbing study of the mystical tradition, *Every Changing Shape* (1964), Jennings announced her concern for "the making of poems, the nature of mystical experience, and the relationship between the two." Beginning with St. Augustine, the volume traces the European tradition from *The Cloud of Unknowing* and Julian of Norwich through T. S. Eliot and Wallace Stevens. The poet-saints of the Spanish baroque, Teresa of Avila and John of the Cross, held a special fascination for her. Jennings, however, lacked the rare capacity for mystical experience. Her mind was too analytical and self-conscious to extinguish itself in wordless union with the divine.

Hungering for deep connection with the divine, Jennings shaped her poetry into a medium that could approximate, if not quite realize, mystical transcendence. As critic Anna Walczuk has argued, Jennings recognized an affinity between poetry and mysticism since both "operate on the principle of joyous rapture and concentration." Jennings believed that both the poet and the mystic seek to describe experiences that are inexpressible in prosaic terms. Jennings understood that she had no religious vocation in the orthodox sense, though she envied priests and nuns in whose consecrated lives "mere breathing is a way to bless." Her romantic entanglements, emotional fragility, and literary ambition impeded the necessary dedication. Her writing, however, assumed the role of a spiritual mission—simultaneously a form of contemplation, prayer, and praise.

Twentieth-century British Catholic literature is an odd and lopsided affair. The novelists stand at the center of the modern tradition. Evelyn Waugh, Graham Greene, Muriel Spark, Anthony Burgess, and J. R. R. Tolkien are canonic authors. By contrast, the poets constitute a motley group of outsiders and eccentrics. G. K. Chesterton, Alfred Noyes, Siegfried Sassoon, Hilaire Belloc, David Jones, Edith Sitwell, George Barker, Peter Levi, George Mackay Brown, and Elizabeth Jennings are not authors much read in college poetry courses, not even at Catholic universities. Aside from a common creed, the poets have no group identity. They shared no aesthetic or cultural vision. Their styles ranged from traditional (Chesterton and Noyes) to experimental (Jones and Sitwell). Their temperaments included the romantic (Noyes), realist (Sassoon), academic (Levi), visionary (Jones), and satiric (Belloc). For many, poetry was a secondary medium. Chesterton and Belloc were primarily prose authors, though their verse was masterful. Jones was a painter. Brown was a novelist and playwright.

What modern British Catholic poets mostly had in common was that they were converts, full of the special zeal and combative energy of Roman *arrivistes*. Some were late-life celebrity converts. Sitwell was baptized at sixty-seven; Sassoon at seventy-one. The few cradle Catholics were an unusual lot—reflecting the English Church's marginal position as the faith of immigrants. Barker, Levi, and Belloc were products of international marriages. Belloc was born in France to an English mother and a French painter. Levi was the son of a Sephardic merchant from Istanbul and an English Catholic mother. (He spent twenty-nine years as a Jesuit before leaving the priesthood to marry.) Half-Irish Barker left the church early, professed atheism, and practiced free love (fathering fifteen children by four women). He reconciled shortly before his death, confessing he had broken every commandment except "Thou Shalt Not Kill." In this curious company, Jennings occupies a singular position simply by being so ordinary. She was a lifelong Catholic from a middle-class English family who earned an undergraduate degree and wrote poems.

The ordinary nature of Jennings's background is crucial in understanding her extraordinary place in English Catholic letters. Born Catholic, she eschewed the personal dramas of conversion that preoccupied many of her Romanized contemporaries. She likewise lacked the visionary fervor of the mystics. Jennings is the poet of quotidian spirituality—a real woman living in real places touched by divine grace. Her religious sense was never detached from her physical senses. Her adult reawakening occurred in Rome, where Christian history took material shape in churches and shrines. The sacred spaces spoke to her soul. Her renewed faith was never fussy and self-dramatizing but a quiet and joyful return to her core identity. One anecdote from her time in Rome illustrates her commonsensical approach. As she climbed the Scala Santa on her knees, Jennings remembered a skeptical priest who doubted that the ancient steps were actually the stairs from Pontius Pilate's *praetorium*, which Christ had mounted to stand trial. It didn't matter, she decided; authentic or not, the shrine was "hallowed by centuries of penitence."

This communitarian sense of Christianity as a mystical body, uniting the living and the dead, enlarged Jennings's vision. Her early work had been intensely individual and personal in its perspective, dominated, she later claimed, "by two overriding themes, self-analysis and a sense of place." Both impulses were refined in Rome. She advanced beyond the purely personal by empathetic observation of other people. Always alert to her sense of place, Jennings now responded to the metaphysical dimensions of her surroundings. "No more poems about foreign cities," Amis declared in 1955, voicing The Movement's insular disdain for the postcard poetry so popular then and now. Although Jennings was a genuine English provincial, contentedly spending her life in Oxford, she never flaunted the Little Englander xenophobia of Amis and Larkin. As a Catholic and intellectual, she saw Rome as a universal and eternal city at the heart of the Western and Christian traditions. Her Italian poems share in this tradition of *urbi et orbi*, local but universal in their ambitions.

Jennings was not a great poet. "Greatness" had no appeal to her. She admired epic visionaries, such as Dante, Milton, or Eliot, who offered sublime visions of civilization and belief. She recognized, however, that her muse was lyric. Jennings's "great" subject was how the individual—fragile, isolated, but alert—negotiated her way through life's difficulties and wonders. Her sensibility was romantic, but her style was neoclassical. The characteristic Jennings poem presents the ache and exhilaration of romantic yearning expressed in exquisitely controlled rhyme and meter. She acknowledges her own confused romantic longings—emotional, artistic, and religious— but subjects them to lucid analysis. Her goal is not to resolve the contradictions but clarify them. Here is her brief poem "Delay":

The radiance of that star that leans on me
Was shining years ago. The light that now
Glitters up there my eye may never see,
And so the time lag teases me with how

Love that loves now may not reach me until
Its first desire is spent. The star's impulse
Must wait for eyes to claim it beautiful
And love arrived may find us somewhere else.

The skillful rhyming, sinuous syntax, and soft metrical beat of the poem—written when the author was in her early twenties—creates such lyric charm that most readers are unprepared for the fatalistic final line. For Jennings, no joy exists untouched by jeopardy. Yet the poem manages both to revel in delicate hope and dismiss it. We indulge in the pleasures of sentiment and stoicism, our emotions mixed like a classic cocktail—bitter spirits plus sweet. Is it any surprise that young Amis, choosing the poem for the university anthology *Oxford Poetry 1949*, crowed to his co-editor that Jennings was "the star of the show, our discovery." Years later Larkin reprinted the poem in his *Oxford Book of Twentieth Century English Verse*, which presented Jennings as one of the major figures of her generation.

Finally, something more needs to be said about Jennings as a woman poet. She never portrayed herself as a feminist, but she wrote from an explicitly female perspective. There is no way to understand her career without seeing how her gender shaped her personal and public identities. She began writing at a time when being female was a grave disadvantage. In the mid-twentieth century, women had an established position in British poetry—second place. They were published but not taken too seriously. The world of letters assumed that men led literary culture. Female poets were typecast as minor lyrists, concerned with personal matters. Tradition assigned men the larger, public themes and more capacious style. These assumptions allowed critics to recognize the more traditional elements in Jennings's work (her elegant lyricism and formal mastery) but miss or misjudge its bolder aspects (her sacramental imagination and lacerating psychological insight).

Women were underrepresented in anthologies and mostly omitted from literary history. If this claim seems exaggerated, look at the leading anthologies of the postwar period. George MacBeth's *Poetry: 1900 to 1965* (1967) contained 21 men and 2 women. Edward-Lucie Smith's *British Poetry Since 1945* (1970) featured 81 men and 6 women. The most influential anthology of the period, Al Alvarez's *The New Poetry* (1962), contained no women at all. When Alvarez revised the volume in 1966, he included 2 women to balance the 26 men. Both of female poets were Americans. No British woman was deemed sufficiently "new." The Movement, which had earlier launched Jennings, consisted of 7 men and 1 woman. It was challenged by "The Group," which included no women at all. This was not a milieu in which women poets received fair critical appraisal.

Jennings's literary reputation never surmounted the limits imposed on women of her generation. By the time of her death in 2001, the situation for female writers had become less grim, but her Catholicism isolated her from the feminist vanguard leading the cultural change. In her later years, reviewers often treated her with condescension and hostility. One young critic mocked her as a "Christian lady" and "emotional anchorite" inhabiting a world of "shapeless woolens, small kindnesses and quiet deaths"—an odious remark even by the snarky standards of British reviewing. Jennings understood the dilemma and bore it, but not without a touch of bitterness. (Few Catholic poets extend the concept of redemptive suffering to include their own bad reviews.)

Catholic iconography portrays martyrs in their heavenly glory displaying the instruments by which they were tortured and killed. St. Sebastian sports his arrows, and St. Catherine slings a friendly arm around her spiked wheel. By the same method, is it possible to understand Jennings's achievement by considering her supposed liabilities as defining virtues? What happens if the standard reservations about her work are rephrased as neutral observations? Let's try.

Jennings was a lyric poet. She mastered short forms. She wrote from an educated woman's perspective. Her work is personal but not blatantly confessional. In a literary era obsessed with style, she focused on content. Her poems cluster around a set of recurring themes—love, religion, art, and relationships. Her poetry reflects her Christian worldview. Her stylistic approach was not to innovate but to perfect. When free verse represented the vanguard, she crafted her signature poems in rhyme and meter. She wrote prolifically.

So stated, the list hardly constitutes an indictment. Essentially, the case against Jennings is that her poetry was different in form and perspective from the sort leading critics preferred. She was not the average professor's idea of a modern poet. Jennings deserves to be judged on her own merits. Her pure and transparent style, her understated mastery of form, her quiet but secure religious convictions, her indifference to literary fashion are what made her work individual. Is it any wonder that she has never lacked readers? Even if one concedes that she wrote too much, it is good to remember Anthony Burgess's notion that artistic devotion "is primarily manifested in prolific production."

Posterity does not judge poets by their average performance. It evaluates their best work and compares it to the tradition. Jennings never wrote the singular, ambitious poem that secured her place in literary history. There is no "Kubla Khan" or "Dover Beach" guarding her place in the anthologies. Instead, she authored dozens of perfect short poems. Like Thomas Hardy, she needs to be read in depth if one is to understand her real achievement. No English poet of her generation, except Larkin, wrote better love poems. In a secular age, she wrote persuasively about religious experience. Her female perspective makes her work meaningfully different from the mostly male canon of modern Christian poetry. It is a modest claim to call her England's finest modern Catholic poet, the competition being so odd and narrow. It is more useful to say that her work returned the Catholic perspective to the mainstream of British verse. Her poetry requires no special pleading either by feminists or Catholics. It speaks for itself with the authority of a classic.

In her poem "Clarify," Jennings prayed:

> Clarify me, please,
> God of the galaxies,
> Make me a meteor,
> Or else a metaphor ...

Isn't it time to answer that prayer, at least in literary terms? Criticism needs to clarify Jennings's significant place in the contemporary canon. Let her life be a metaphor of artistic dedication, held bravely against the odds. Her poems flash like meteors illuminating what it means to be human.

II

If Any Fire Endures Beyond Its Flame: A Conversation With Dana Gioia

(*Christianity & Literature,* 2006)
By Robert Lance Snyder

RLS:

In God and the Imagination: On Poets, Poetry, and the Ineffable *(2002), Paul Mariani quotes the concluding lines of Wallace Stevens's "Final Soliloquy of the Interior Paramour":*

> Here, now, we forget each other and ourselves.
> We feel the obscurity of an order, a whole,
> A knowledge, that which arranged the rendezvous,
>
> Within its vital boundary, in the mind.
> We say God and the imagination are one . . .
> How high that highest candle lights the dark.

Mariani states that the passage indicates this poet's "self-humbling before the Sublime," but he also points out how shiftily evasive is the Modernist qualifier "We say" in the line: "We say God and the imagination are one." How do you construe Stevens here? Are God and the imagination one?

DG:

Stevens's splendid "Final Soliloquy of the Interior Paramour" is one of his last poems, written after a lifetime of meditation on the problematic meaning of existence in a world without God. Stevens tried to posit the human imagination as an adequate substitute for divinity. He developed a complex and subtle worldview in which all values were created by the human imagination.

On his deathbed, however, Stevens reportedly asked the hospital chaplain to baptize him into the Catholic Church. Once you ponder that spiritual decision in the face of death—which is at once both extraordinary and commonplace—you notice that Stevens's late poetry is saturated with his longing for faith in some transcendent reality. I would, therefore, interpret Stevens's famous line in light of his own spiritual journey. It is not the ironic utterance of an atheistic aesthete. It is an existential gesture of hope by a profoundly reflective man standing on the threshold of death—a philosophical poet looking from the outermost border of reason across great vistas of mystery.

What did Stevens mean when he wrote, "God and the imagination are one"? As the Modernist most deeply engaged in the Romantic tradition, Stevens saw the imagination as both a creative and cognitive force, but he must have suspected that the human mind was not an adequate substitute for God. At the end of his life, did he recognize the imagination as a pathway to divinity? Such a Wordsworthian a view of Stevens is not implausible—if one takes the account of his baptism seriously.

RLS:

Elsewhere in his book Mariani cites Stevens's observation, "One of the visible movements of the modern imagination is the movement away from God." He then proposes that the statement "suggests its corollary— as the subtle master well knew—that one of the invisible *movements of the modern imagination may therefore be* toward *that same God." What evidence do you see in contemporary poetry, and more broadly in the arts, that might corroborate this hypothesis?*

DG:

I find Mariani too hopeful here. Modernity has effectively secularized culture and society. Contemporary consumer culture not only makes the individual the center of value; it also caters to the lowest elements of human nature—greed, vanity, gluttony, lust, and sloth. Conformity, complacency, and creature comforts hardly represent the ideals of a great culture. They may be economically powerful motives, but they inhibit any genuine spiritual development. In a healthier culture the arts would stand in opposition to these forces of vulgarity, triviality, and excess, but in contemporary culture the arts increasingly reflect them. Our culture has largely lost its sense of the sacred.

RLS:

Which poets writing today do you think of as being religious or, more specifically, Christian?

DG:

Most poets consider themselves "spiritual" in some sense, but there are few American poets today who write from a specifically religious perspective, and fewer poets still who write especially well from such conviction. The best religious poet now active in the U.S. is surely Richard Wilbur, who may also be our best living poet *tout court*. His work is deeply Christian, permeated by a spiritual joy unusual for modern religious poetry. He has no peers among contemporary American religious poets. Equally distinguished is the poetry of Charles Causley, a Cornish writer who died in 2003. Idiosyncratic, visionary, and unabashedly musical, his verse combines mystery and immediacy in ways hard to describe. He somehow married the forms of traditional ballad and popular song with the sensibility of surrealism—half Bob Dylan, half William Blake.

Then there is the dense, dour, and magnificent Geoffrey Hill. He is not to everyone's liking. He is a poet's poet's poet. But Hill rewards study. Other interesting contemporary Christian poets include Marilyn Nelson, Jody Bottum, Kathleen Norris, and Robert B. Shaw. Then there is an interesting Christian poetry of doubt in writers such as X. J. Kennedy, Andrew Hudgins, and Mark Jarman.

RLS:

Have these contemporaries influenced your own work or sense of poetic vocation?

DG:

Not significantly. I adore Wilbur's poetry, but his sense of language and religious experience is curiously distant from my own. He writes English of enormous originality, with an ear greatly influenced by French. His most direct impact has been to remind me that lyric perfection is still possible today. Causley has had a little more influence—mostly in his gift of mixing the mundane and the magical. Hill's work is remote from my own practice, though I admire the density of his language and the authenticity of his spiritual struggle.

The Christian poets who influence me most deeply came from an earlier generation—T. S. Eliot and W. H. Auden. I read them both in early adolescence, and they have exerted a constant influence on both my poetry and criticism. In recent years they have also shaped my sense of verse theater and operatic drama. Auden is my favorite modern poet. Eliot is surely the greatest modern critic, though Auden's more casual criticism is nearly as fine and much more compassionate.

RLS:

What about the presence of Christianity in other arts?

DG:

There has been a great revival of sacred music in the last twenty years. Two composers of genius I would recommend are Arvo Pärt and Morten Lauridsen. Pärt, an Estonian, is now a figure of international stature. He has fundamentally reinvented sacred music for our time, incorporating elements of Medieval, Renaissance, and Eastern Orthodox vocal writing in a minimalist but deeply expressive manner. His importance at the moment is hard to overstate. Lauridsen is less prolific, but his *Lux Aeterna* is one of the few true masterpieces of recent American music. Other significant sacred composers include Henri Gorecki, Osvaldo Golijov, Dave Brubeck, James MacMillan, Gavin Bryars, and John Tavener.

RLS:

Let me ask you about two different notions of poetic language. Certain poets seem to discover through language a power of disclosure, unveiling, or unconcealment, whereas others appear to take that dimension of aletheia *for granted. If this distinction makes sense, how do you conceive of explicitly Christian faith as functioning in the writing of poetry?*

DG:

This is an important distinction, but both attitudes toward language have poetic potential. The first poem in my third collection, *Interrogations at Noon*, is called "Words." The final poem is "Unsaid." Both poems discuss the limits of language—what can be said about the world and what cannot be expressed. Both are very Catholic poems, although there is nothing overtly religious in either work.

The relationship between language and reality is a fundamental question for any serious poet. That relationship differs profoundly for a Christian and a postmodernist skeptic. My basic view of lyric poetry is both sacramental and metaphysical. It is not enough to show the surface of the world or the exterior of existence. It is also necessary to reveal, or at least suggest, what lies beyond the physical senses. The relation between the visible and the invisible is an inevitable theme for the poet.

RLS:

In all your collections to date one detects a pervasively elegiac undertone related to what April Lindner, commenting specifically on Daily Horoscope, *describes as "themes of loss and displacement," a "sense of exile from essential things." Would you kindly reflect on whence that "sense of exile" arises?*

DG:

The notion of exile has always been present in my life. I was raised in an immigrant family in an immigrant neighborhood. There were Italians, Mexicans, Cubans, Filipinos, Vietnamese, Japanese, and Chinese around me every day. Almost everyone's family had been forced to leave its homeland by poverty or persecution. Even the native-born Americans had mostly fled the Dust Bowl. Everyone had come seeking a new life—at the cost of an old one. Exile was never an abstraction in mid-century Los Angeles. It was our common background.

My adult life has been a series of exiles—from the place, family, language, and social class of my childhood. They were voluntary but nonetheless exacted a great personal cost. The first move was the shortest in physical distance but the biggest in impact. I left working-class Latin Los Angeles for the privileged environs of Stanford University. Since then I have lived in Vienna, Boston, New York, Rome, Minneapolis, San Francisco, and now Washington, D.C. My family and relatives have usually been far away. How could that not affect my poetry?

RLS:

In Daily Horoscope *motifs of loss have both personal and cultural dimensions. Poems such as "California Hills in August," "In Chandler Country," "Eastern Standard Time," and "In Cheever Country" chronicle your own transcontinental migration and memory-forged impression of "feeling out of place." Other poems in* Daily Horoscope, *however, seem to universalize the experience. I am thinking especially of "Waiting in the Airport," a poem that incisively dramatizes the anonymity of what Marc Augé has referred to as the "non-places" so predominant in "super-modernity." Do you consider such displacement as merely symptomatic of our age or as endemic to human existence?*

DG:

The themes of loss and displacement are central to lyric poetry. They arise naturally from the human condition—from the recognition of our mortality and the irresistible ravages of time. As Stevens observed, "Death is the mother of beauty." If we were all immortal, there would be no need for poetry. No need for any sort of art or philosophy. Look at how petty, vain, and self-indulgent the gods in Homer are—worse than a Hollywood bratpack.

I am a Latin Catholic—a mixture of Italian and Mexican. I was raised by working people who had been born in poverty and suffered enormous losses in their lives. My mother's childhood was a nightmare of deprivation. My family had a stoical view of existence. You bore your sorrows quietly. When I read Seneca and Marcus Aurelius in college, I felt an immediate sense of recognition. Their voices sounded like my Sicilian uncles and grandfather. Stoicism is the Mediterranean and Mexican worldview.

RLS:

Is displacement, then, merely part of the human condition?

DG:

Displacement has always been a factor in human existence, but historically it has mostly been an exceptional condition that arose out of dire circumstances like war, plague, famine, or natural disaster. Most people wanted lives of human continuity, deeply rooted in a particular place, clan, faith, and culture. Modernity and America have created situations where displacement is necessary for success and upward mobility. The average American moves every seven years— often thousands of miles. Children are raised hardly knowing their grandparents or extended family. Neighborhoods are torn down and rebuilt. Families split up. Old people retire in places where they have never lived. The mobility of our society has greatly contributed to our material prosperity, but it has enormous human cost.

RLS:

I am curious about the voice deployed in the title sequence of Daily Horoscope. *On the one hand, the omniscient speaker asserts that "nothing is hidden in the obvious / changes of the world," but shortly thereafter we are urged to "look toward earth" rather than the zodiac for evidence of "another world":*

> Look for smaller signs instead, the fine
> disturbances of ordered things when suddenly
> the rhythms of your expectation break
> and in a moment's pause another world
> reveals itself behind the ordinary.

How are we to reconcile these two divergent views?

DG:

I try not to interpret my own poems for two reasons. First, if the poem is any good, it should convey its own meanings. (If the poem isn't any good, then who cares what it means?) Second, I feel that I have no monopoly on saying what a poem of mine means or doesn't mean. Having published a poem, I become only one of its readers. I may remember things about its origins, but I am also likely to be blind to other aspects of the final work. I may know what I intended but not what I actually created.

RLS:

But will you nonetheless say something about the seemingly divergent views expressed in this poem?

DG:

I don't want my poems to provide answers. I want them to pose questions worth pondering. My sequence "Daily Horoscope" is a conversation—a series of arguments in soliloquy. Most of my poems proceed this way. I can't write more than a few lines without shifting the mood or arguing with myself. The structure of lyric poetry is dialectical. Isn't that how thoughts or emotions unfold—up and down, back and forth? Consciousness never moves in a straight line.

RLS:

What appears to be at stake in "Daily Horoscope" is the idea of immanence, as well as the concept of aletheia. *Would you agree?*

DG:

Yes, immanence and *aletheia* are motives in "Daily Horoscope," though I might have described these themes using slightly different terms. Those are among the issues that the poem argues about.

RLS:

I would like to invoke Robert McPhillips's canny judgment that your work is "marked by a distinctive poetic style of visionary realism in which memory imbues details of the ordinary world with a sensuous luminosity, making them at once seemingly tangible yet tantalizingly elusive, as if existing in a border region between time and eternity." Does the creative act itself effect for you an epiphanic passage through what McPhillips terms "a border region between time and eternity," or what in "Song from a Courtyard Window" you refer to as "that strange place / that's always changing, constantly drifting / between the visible and invisible"?

DG:

For me, most poems begin as a small epiphany. Some ordinary object or event makes a small rip in the fabric of time and place, and I sense something lying beyond. The passage you quoted earlier from "Daily Horoscope" could describe the beginning of my own creative process. For me, inspiration has always been involuntary—sudden, surprising, and often disturbing. The finished poem attempts to recreate that experience of awe and wonder.

RLS:

The Gods of Winter *is dedicated to the memory of your first son, Michael Jasper Gioia, who died in December 1987 at four months of age. In a 1992 interview you admitted that after this grievous loss you "saw poetry differently": "Writing took on a spiritual urgency I had never experienced before." Would you please elaborate?*

DG:

After my first son's death I fell into a terrible period of grief, which was prolonged and intensified by several other family deaths. I kept reaching for poetry but found that very little writing, especially contemporary poetry, could reach me. It seemed mostly trivial, self-absorbed, and pointlessly clever. I needed poetry strong enough to bear the weight of my emotions. I stopped writing for nearly a year. When I started writing again, I put different demands on my work. I wanted my poems to concern things of consequence. I also wanted them to be true—not platitudinously true like so much political or devotional poetry but to work assiduously toward grasping difficult fundamental truths of human existence.

RLS:

Did this experience change your sense of an audience?

DG:

It broadened my sense of audience. I knew that I had to resist the constant pressure nowadays to write for a coterie audience of poets and critics. My poetry is deeply literary—carefully written, informed by tradition, full of allusion—but I do not write solely for the literati.

I try to engage any alert and intelligent reader or listener. I attempt to make the surface of the poem, whether of sound or story, as arresting as possible so that the other elements do their work on a subconscious or semi-conscious level.

RLS:

In the opening section of The Gods of Winter, *"All Souls'," "Veterans' Cemetery," and "The Gods of Winter" explore the blank sense of nullity that overtakes one upon great personal tragedy, but the section closes with "Planting a Sequoia" and a poignant rite:*

> *But today we kneel in the cold planting you, our native giant,*
> *Defying the practical custom of our fathers,*
> *Wrapping in your roots a lock of hair, a piece of an infant's birth cord,*
> *All that remains above earth of a first-born son,*
> *A few stray atoms brought back to the elements.*

Is the writing of such an autobiographical poem, which memorializes the act of memorializing, part of what you understand Robert Hayden to mean by "love's austere and lonely offices," which you quote as an epigraph to your book's second section?

DG:

"Planting a Sequoia" is one of the few entirely autobiographical poems I have ever published. Most of my poems are fictional to a greater or lesser degree. The events in "Planting a Sequoia" actually happened as described in the poem. I shaped the narrative only by dropping a few unnecessary details. I wanted the poem to commemorate my son as a living presence and not merely grieve over his death. What is an elegy except a poem that tries to "memorialize the act of memorializing?"

RLS:

"Counting the Children," the first of two long narrative poems in The Gods of Winter, *develops further your meditation on mortality. The poem presents Mr. Choi, an "accountant sent out by the State / To take an inventory of the house" in which a wealthy woman died intestate. Arriving at the dead woman's home, he is ushered into a bedroom containing shelf after shelf of discarded dolls that have been sorted by kind. Witnessing this silent horde, Mr. Choi wonders: "Was this where all lost childhoods go?" He then is terrified by a dream that bodes his daughter's death unless he can prevent ledger numbers from "slipping down the page, / Suddenly breaking up like Scrabble letters / Brushed into a box to end a game," and "find the sum." This nightmare section soon modulates toward a visionary conclusion. What was the source of this poem?*

DG:

"Counting the Children" was based on a real incident—a madwoman's ramshackle private museum I happened to visit years ago in rural Alabama. ("Guide to the Other Gallery," another poem in *The Gods of Winter*, also borrowed details from this eerie museum.) At first I drafted a short lyric poem, but it didn't convey the overwhelming weirdness of the place. I decided to recast the experience in a narrative. I gradually created a story and a narrator in which to relocate the image of this woman's macabre, terrifying doll collection.

The story took on a life of its own and expanded beyond my original idea. I was working on this poem when my son died. When I resumed writing many months later, I radically revised the poem and added the final section. I looked to Dante for both the form and the narrative structure. I had initially written about hell. I decided to continue the narrator's journey through purgatory and at least give a glimpse into paradise. I don't mention Dante anywhere in the poem, and the reader needn't catch the allusion to understand the story. But if you notice the Dantean correspondences, other layers of meaning become apparent.

RLS:

Let me ask another question about "Counting the Children." Years later, having "learned the loneliness that we call love," Mr. Choi no longer worries—his daughter is now seven—but has a vision concerning which he asks:

> *What if completion comes only in beginnings?*
> *The naked tree exploding into flower?*
> *And all our prim assumptions about time*
>
> *Prove wrong? What if we cannot read the future*
> *Because our destiny moves back in time,*
> *And only memory speaks prophetically?*

I am intrigued by the conditional clause in the final lines. How is it that "our destiny moves back in time, / And only memory speaks prophetically"?

DG:

We tend to think of destiny moving from the present into the future, but it moves more powerfully from the past toward the present. Isn't this a central truth for Christians? We look back toward the Redemption, which wouldn't have been possible without the Incarnation. And to answer why the Incarnation was necessary, we must go all the way back to the Garden of Eden. The future is the past unfolding into the present. The same thing is true of us biologically. We are the sum total of our genetic inheritance.

RLS:

Your poetry is rarely overtly religious, yet there is a constant sense of spiritual struggle in your work. Why is it that religion becomes an explicit subject in only a few instances?

DG:

With the exception of a few short poems like "The Burning Ladder," "The Litany," or "The Archbishop," my poems seldom have religion as their overt subject. My verse, however, is deeply theological. The most specifically Christian works I have written tend to be my long ones—the narrative poems in *The Gods of Winter* and *Daily Horoscope* as well as my two libretti, *Nosferatu* and *Tony Caruso's Final Broadcast*. If you read "The Room Upstairs," "Counting the Children," and "The Homecoming," you will see what I mean. The poems are not in any sense devotional, but they dramatize aspects of the Christian mythos, especially the journey from despair to grace, from confusion to redemption. Or in the case of "The Homecoming" they portray evil—the choice of sin and the refusal of grace. "The Homecoming" is essentially a theological poem about the nature of evil and free will. As for my two libretti, they contain overtly religious elements and even incorporate portions of Catholic liturgy.

RLS:

Why is it that the narrative rather than lyric form proves more conducive for you in composing poems that deal with such Christian mysteries as grace and our response to it?

DG:

Lyric poetry need only convey the feelings and insights of an instant. It may hint at broader meaning, but there is no obligation to provide a fuller account of human existence. The poet needs only to create "a moment's monument." A single small insight expressed in memorably beautiful language is enough to sustain a lyric. A narrative poem, however, needs to depict something far more extensive—a significant action along with its motives and consequences. There is no way to convey the significance of an action, neither its motives nor consequences, without being alert to its morality.

As I began working on narrative poems thirty years ago, I faced a series of problems. The tradition of verse narrative was officially dead. Writers were supposed to use prose for telling stories. There were almost no viable contemporary models for poetic narrative. Modernism had mostly rejected narrative poetry in favor of the lyric mode. A few poets had attempted cumbersome book-length epic works—usually cluttered with cultural content and lacking in narrative momentum. Those poems didn't offer much help. I needed to find a style at once flexible enough to tell a story but still capable of poetic force and lyric resonance.

RLS:

What solution did you bring to this dilemma?

DG:

The essential thing was to tell a compelling story of moral consequence. Something of life-or-death importance had to be at the heart of the poem. Otherwise it was hard to build a work of sufficient intensity that transformed narrative verse into real poetry. I gradually came to realize that the most compelling stories had some mythic resonance. As Geoffrey Hill wrote, "No bloodless myth will hold." Reaching that deep resonance inevitably brings out a writer's core beliefs. In my case that meant the mythos, signs, and symbols of Catholicism.

None of this was conscious on my part. It just happened as the poems developed. The mythic elements inherently and unconsciously arose out of the subjects. You can't write about what is important without revealing your own values and beliefs.

RLS:

Your work, especially the narrative poems, seems fascinated by the idea of evil. Needless to say, this is not a common theme in our relativistic age. Why does evil play such a significant role in your work?

DG:

I believe in evil. I believe some people choose evil because it frees them from moral restraints and gives them power over others. In most cases, choosing evil is not a matter of ignorance. These people usually know that they are doing wrong, no matter how they later try to justify or excuse their actions. Neither Hitler nor Stalin would have become a just and humane ruler had he taken a seminar on ethics. Their corruption was a matter of will. They chose cruelty and evil as a road to power. I am archaic enough to believe in sin. Why else do we need redemption? I deal with these questions most explicitly in "The Homecoming" and *Nosferatu*, but they haunt many of my poems.

RLS:

Am I correct in seeing the devil, or at least demonic figures, present in your poems?

DG:

With Marlowe, Milton, Dante, and Goethe among my favorite writers, how can I resist introducing the devil? Sometimes he is present quite explicitly as in *Nosferatu*. Sometimes he is there implicitly, as in the poem "Guide to the Other Gallery," which is narrated by a demon in hell. Flannery O'Connor showed the compelling possibilities of introducing the demonic into the mundane, just as T. S. Eliot and Baudelaire demonstrated ways to bring hell into the modern city.

RLS:

You seem to make the demonic figures in your work articulate and persuasive characters. Does this risk glorifying evil?

DG:

It is an interesting poetic challenge to give voice to evil. Milton and Marlowe understood that you have to give the devil the best lines. How else can you make his unpleasant notions seductive? If you want to create the dramatic and narrative power to sustain a work that examines these moral issues seriously, you must create a real struggle between good and evil. Too many contemporary writers can't create plausible villains. Perhaps they are unwilling to recognize their own potential for evil, which is probably necessary to create some sense of authenticity. A poet must give the devil his due.

RLS:

Between "Counting the Children" and "The Homecoming" in The Gods of Winter *are ten very diverse poems. At least four ("News from Nineteen Eighty-Four," "The Silence of the Poets," "My Confessional Sestina," "Money") demonstrate a more public voice emerging in the collection. Your books seem consciously arranged in contrasting suites of poems. When so many contemporary poets strive for books with a unitary style and thematics, why do you prefer such diversity?*

DG:

I consider variety an important poetic virtue. I generally find it dull to read a book in which all of the poems are alike in mood, form, and style—unless the book is an integrated sequence like Meredith's *Modern Love* or Rilke's *Sonnets to Orpheus*. I especially prize formal and musical variety. Since poets cannot choose their own imaginative obsessions—those tend to be involuntary—they can at least strive for different forms of expression. One reason I so greatly admire W. H. Auden, Weldon Kees, Elizabeth Bishop, and Philip Larkin is their versatility. Despite the powerful sense of individual personality in their work, their poems are so often surprising in shape, length, or mood.

I strive for diversity of expressive means. In *Interrogations at Noon* I wrote poems in almost every English measure except syllabics. I even used triple meters and strong-stress verse. No critic noticed, at least in print, but I like to think many readers felt and enjoyed the variety unconsciously.

RLS:

I want to ask about a shorter poem in The Gods of Winter *that attests to something far deeper than ordinary rapprochement with the immediacy of grief. "On Approaching Forty" describes, in the first person, a midlife transformation motivated by suffering and sorrow. The poem concludes:*

> *The years rise like a swarm around my shoulders.*
> *Nothing has been in vain. This is the work*
> *which all complete together and alone,*
> *the living and the dead, to penetrate*
> *the impenetrable world, down open roads,*
> *down mineshafts of discovery and loss,*
> *and learned from many loves or only one,*
> *from father down to son—till all is clear.*

> *And having said this, I can start out now,*
> *easy in the eternal company*
> *of all things living, of all things dead,*
> *to disappear in either dust or fire*
> *if any fire endures beyond its flame.*

In these magnificent lines is registered, obviously, a new stage of spiritual insight and acceptance, one whose expression reverberates with all kinds of scriptural as well as literary echoes. Might I invite you to comment on this passage in light of my observation?

DG:

"On Approaching Forty" is a translation from the Modernist Italian poet, Mario Luzi, so I did not invent the situation or imagery, though I freely recreated it in English. What drew me to Luzi's poem are exactly the qualities you mention. Luzi shares my admiration for T. S. Eliot, especially his use of liturgical language and sacramental symbolism. My translation is also alert to something deeply embedded in Luzi's poem—the Augustinian notion of the Communion of the Saints that unites the living and the dead. "On Approaching Forty" is a deeply Catholic poem. I should have mentioned Luzi earlier in this interview when you asked about contemporary Christian poets. Luzi died at ninety in 2005. He was one of the great Christian poets of the past century—an Italian equivalent to T. S. Eliot.

RLS:

Much of what I see as your poetic integrity in The Gods of Winter *derives from its fifth and final section. Rather than extrapolating the recognition that "Nothing has been in vain" into a homiletic valediction, you instead trace the difficulty of endurance after an irreversible loss. "Becoming a Redwood" harks back to "Planting a Sequoia" and posits that healing "change is possible," while "Maze Without a Minotaur" speaks of the impulse to "raze each suffocating room" of remembrance. In this context "Speaking of Love" conveys powerfully the parental survivors' struggle to surmount the impasse of denial and silence, which "can become its own cliché," in the wake of "How little there seemed left to us." The work's final lines, however, are suffused with ambivalence, if not something darker:*

> *And so at last we speak again of love,*
> *Now that there is nothing left unsaid,*
> *Surrendering our voices to the past,*
> *Which has betrayed us. Each of us alone,*
> *Obsessed by memory, befriended by desire,*
>
> *With no words left to summon back our love.*

Because this passage anticipates the coda of Interrogations at Noon, *would you address what it describes? Certainly more is involved here than what Emily Dickinson communicates in writing that "After great pain, a formal feeling comes."*

DG:

Once again I hesitate to offer interpretations of my own poems, especially when you so capably demonstrate your own understanding of them. Let me say only that "Speaking of Love" portrays the fragility of language—how easily it can be exhausted, cheapened, or misused. When language is debased, then all the essential things we need it for—love, learning, communication, ritual—are threatened and weakened. The poem also reflects the sad truth that we often despoil or destroy things without intending to.

As for my resisting the homiletic and valedictory impulses, I hope you are right. I want my poems to express ideas but not in any neat or modular way. I admire poetry that conveys hard wisdom won from and still inseparable from experience. The impulse of my poetry originates mostly in mystery, anxiety, and uncertainty. If something can be stated unequivocally and unambiguously, I see no purpose or pleasure in saying it in poetry.

RLS:

To what extent do you regard the trauma of loss and the experience of despair as essential to the life of faith?

DG:

Some people may be lucky enough to lead lives untouched by pain, loss, struggle, and despair. I am not one of them. My life has been enormously difficult—full of physical, emotional, and spiritual pain. Some people may also be able to learn life's lessons effortlessly. Not me. I have done many stupid and destructive things. I may be a quick study for intellectual things, but whatever real wisdom I possess came slowly and painfully. I would not have learned much about humility, compassion, patience, and generosity if suffering had not so often instructed me.

RLS:

Do you consider suffering, then, a necessary element for spiritual growth?

DG:

Isn't suffering central to Christianity? Certainly the Mediterranean Latin Catholicism I was raised in was based on the unavoidable but redemptive nature of suffering. The Stations of the Cross, the Rosary, and the Lives of the Saints were all meditations on the centrality of suffering to spiritual development. I was taught to bear pain quietly. If you accept suffering, it teaches you courage, patience, and compassion. If you refuse to bear life's inevitable pain, you become bitter, resentful, and self-pitying. Properly accepted, suffering is a gift.

RLS:

Having already alluded to "Unsaid," with which Interrogations at Noon *ends, I would like to pose a question about the book's opening poem, "Words," which begins by admitting:*

> *The world does not need words. It articulates itself*
> *in sunlight, leaves, and shadows. The stones on the path*
> *are no less real for lying uncatalogued and uncounted.*
> *The fluent leaves speak only the dialect of pure being.*
> *The kiss is still fully itself though no words were spoken.*

However, if language is superfluous to nature, which speaks "only the dialect of pure being," words clearly transform our experience of the world:

Yet the stones remain less real to those who cannot
name them, or read the mute syllables graven in silica.
To see a red stone is less than seeing it as jasper —
metamorphic quartz, cousin to the flint the Kiowa
carved as arrowheads. To name is to know and remember.

In a vein reminiscent of Gerard Manley Hopkins, you then close the
poem by writing, "The daylight needs no praise, and so we praise it
always — / greater than ourselves and all the airy words we summon."
How for you is poetry a vehicle of praise?

DG:

Rilke once asserted that the role of the poet was to praise. When I
first read his poem "Praise" as an undergraduate, I thought it was
merely a literary pose. I now realize that I was wrong. The central
purpose of poetry is to praise existence — without, of course, deny-
ing the harsher realities. Rilke understood that difficult spiritual
truth, ultimately the same lesson that Job learned at the end of his
suffering. Wisdom comes from seeing and accepting reality — from
understanding the vast beauty of creation and our own humble
place in it. If poetry is to be a vehicle of truth and discovery, and not
merely a pleasing fiction, then it must see, love, and praise the world,
not as we imagine it but as it truly is.

I am not saying that poetry must be optimistic or upbeat. Absolutely
not! Nothing depresses me more in poetry than "uplift." Poetry must
deal with suffering, loss, despair, and death, but it needs to see them
in the broadest context as the necessary preconditions of enlightenment, grace, and redemption. How can we understand the good
without experiencing evil or appreciate joy without first knowing
pain? I have sat by the deathbeds of both my parents and watched
them die. I have held the dead body of my little son in my arms. That
is how I learned to appreciate the unimaginably great gift of being
alive.

The concept of praise also emerges in "The Litany." If I am correct in regarding the collection overall as examining, from a Dantean midpoint or figurative "noon" in life, the specious illusions we weave about our lives, then "The Litany" strikes me as profoundly central to the work as a whole.

DG:

"The Litany" is one of the central poems in *Interrogations at Noon*. It is also probably the most difficult poem in the book. It is easy to misunderstand if you focus on any one part out of context. The poem needs to be read as a progressive journey or argument in which each part rejects or qualifies what came before.

RLS:

What I wish to ask concerning this poem requires an explanatory prologue. "The Litany" begins by announcing that it will be an inventory:

> *This is a litany of lost things,*
> *a canon of possessions dispossessed,*
> *a photograph, an old address, a key.*
> *It is a list of words to memorize*
> *or to forget—of amo, amas, amat,*
> *the conjugations of a dead tongue*
> *in which the final sentence has been spoken.*

By the third stanza these tropes of our attachment to "lost things" belonging to a memorialized past give way to the persona's barren offering of "a prayer to unbelief," his resistance to spiritual divestiture making even the Crucifixion appear a blasphemous parody of the sacrifice necessary for atonement:

It is the smile of a stone Madonna
and the silent fury of the consecrated wine,
a benediction on the death of a young god,
brave and beautiful, rotting on a tree.

A turn occurs, however, in the ensuing memento mori. *With its mandate to savor "the bitterness of earth and ashes," the poem takes us beyond captivity by "time's / illusions" toward a vision of "pure paradox"—the apprehension of "our life" as a "shattered river rising as it falls." Reading this incantatory poem, I cannot help but think of Eliot's* Four Quartets, *the second movement of which ("East Coker") proclaims "the way of dispossession," associated with the apophatic tradition within Christianity, as the path to a redemptive understanding of human existence. Would you grant this suggestion of a parallel? My question stems in part from your fourth stanza's declaration that "This is a prayer to praise what we become, / 'Dust thou art, to dust thou shalt return.'"*

DG:

"The Litany" may parallel Eliot's "East Coker" in some respects, but I did not have *Four Quartets* in mind when I wrote the poem. What you are sensing is our common roots in Catholic ritual and Christian mysticism. As for the apophatic tradition, one of the most effective means of lyric poetry is apophasis. This is especially true of religious poetry, which cannot literally show the subjects it purports to present. Likewise all lyric poetry is in some sense a *memento mori* since its intensity depends on a sense of our mortality and the irreversible flow of time.

I began sketching out "The Litany" at the same time I wrote "Planting a Sequoia," but I had trouble getting beyond the opening. I couldn't figure out the shape the poem needed to take. I knew the poem had to create a powerful musical spell, but the melody eluded me. I couldn't even decide whether the poem should be in meter or free verse. I kept jotting down lines and playing with stanza patterns for several years before I figured out the right rhythm for the lines and images. Once I finally hammered out the opening stanza, the rest

146

of the poem came at once. Something that "The Litany" does borrow from Eliot is a technical element from his early work in *vers libre*—the intricate maneuvers of a poem moving around "the ghost of a meter," slipping in and out of form.

RLS:

Another poem in Interrogations at Noon, *"A California Requiem," seems closely linked to "The Litany." "A California Requiem" begins with the speaker's surveying a contemporary West Coast cemetery:*

> I walked among the equidistant graves
> New planted in the irrigated lawn.
> The square, trim headstones quietly declared
> The impotence of grief against the sun.
>
> There were no outward signs of human loss.
> No granite angel wept beside the lane.
> No bending willow broke the once-rough ground
> Now graded to a geometric plane.
>
> My blessèd California, you are so wise.
> You render death abstract, efficient, clean.
> Your afterlife is only real estate,
> And in his kingdom Death must stay unseen.

The speaker then hears the whispered confession of those interred there. What the chorus of ghostly voices intones is a shared failure. Those who "claimed the earth but did not hear her claim" while alive seek now to earn "Forgiveness from the lives we dispossessed." Disinherited by what they have despoiled and cannot even name, these self-portrayed shadows that "the bright noon erases" can only shrink back into the void they created by shunning the fact of mortality. Could you say something about this striking poem?

There was a tradition in Medieval and Renaissance literature of the vision poem, often an allegorical narrative in which the protagonist is given a supernatural vision. The vision could be of the past, the future, the afterlife, or something else not normally open to human scrutiny. *The Vision Concerning Piers Plowman* and Dante's *Commedia* are two famous examples of this religious literary genre. "A California Requiem" seeks to rehabilitate this venerable but neglected genre in a contemporary setting.

Obviously the vision presented in "A California Requiem" is rooted in the ecological disaster of my native state, but it also borrows a moral premise from Dante. Early in the *Inferno* Dante depicts vacillating crowds of souls in Limbo—the lost souls—who were neither good nor bad. Even hell won't let them enter. I borrowed this curious theological notion for my poem. These souls had never been truly alive, and so they can't truly die. It's pure heresy, I know, but the premise opened up certain poetic possibilities. I was disappointed that the Vatican recently dismissed the concept of Limbo. I don't dispute their theology, but I felt Limbo was a place I had actually seen.

RLS:

In contrast to the stark outlook of "A California Requiem," "The Lost Garden" limns an alternative reaction to "The Litany": If "the old estate" of prelapsarian innocence has been forfeited, a compensatory principle is still operative:

> *The trick is making memory a blessing,*
> *To learn by loss subtraction of desire,*
> *Of wanting nothing more than what has been,*
> *To know the past forever lost, yet seeing*
> *Behind the wall a garden still in blossom.*

How is this "trick" of "making memory a blessing" actually wrought in the living of one's life? Extending the query further, is it also something that for you occurs during, or perhaps accrues from, the process of writing poetry?

DG:

The trick of making memory a blessing is twofold. First, one needs to recognize that everything that happens in life, even the hardest things, when seen from the proper perspective, is a gift. Every loss bestows its blessing, if one is humble or patient enough to receive it. Second, memory and imagination constitute our human means of conquering time and mortality. Memory allows one to revisit lost places and lost people. If one can resist the powerful urge to regret and mourn—and there is a period of grief after any deep loss when such resistance is impossible—then one can recapture an enormous amount of the past. "What thou lovest well remains," as Ezra Pound said, and "the rest is dross." I often converse with the dead.

RLS:

Many of your poems in Interrogations at Noon *are adaptations, variations, or imitations of other writers, among them Rainer Maria Rilke ("Entrance"), Constantine Cavafy ("After a Line by Cavafy"), Seneca ("Descent to the Underworld" and "Juno Plots Her Revenge"), and Valerio Magrelli ("Homage to Valerio Magrelli"). With the sole exception of Weldon Kees ("Lives of the Great Composers") in* Daily Horoscope, *however, the same is not true for your earlier two collections. Is this simply a reflection of the fact that throughout the 1990s you were committed to various other projects, including translations of Seneca's* The Madness of Hercules *and Eugenio Montale's* Mottetti *and composition of the libretto for Alva Henderson's opera* Nosferatu? *Or might this interest in translation and adaptation suggest that you increasingly have come to recognize that your creative voice has been inflected by that of others?*

DG:

Although my third volume contained more translations than the earlier books, it wasn't as radical a change as you suggest. *The Gods of Winter* contained versions of Rilke, Luzi, and Nina Cassian. I included these particular translations because I felt that each of the three poems—from German, Italian, and Romanian—had been successfully transformed into an English-language poem with a theme and style almost indistinguishable from my own. There were no translations in *Daily Horoscope*, but the book did include poems that directly drew from other literary texts. "In Chandler Country" borrows the voice of the detective Philip Marlowe from Raymond Chandler. "In Cheever Country" is an homage to the landscape and milieu of John Cheever. "My Secret Life" is a commentary on the Victorian memoir of that title. These poems all appropriated or argued with literary works, though their sources were all prose works. I simply used translation and allusion more overtly in *Interrogations at Noon* than in earlier books. In writing this way, I'm not just acknowledging my literary sources but also calling attention to the nature of poetry.

RLS:

How do these translations and adaptations call attention to the nature of poetry?

DG:

Poetry achieves its particular resonance by playing off the reader's experience with tradition. By "tradition" I don't mean any monolithic literary canon but rather the reader's total previous engagement with all sorts of literary texts—from nursery rhymes and popular songs to classic poems and novels. Those works set up a network of expectations and associations that provide contrasts and comparisons. Whether in its form or genre, subject or rhetoric, image or diction, the new poem engages and exploits the reader's experience.

A strong poem compels the reader to readjust his or her interior sense of things to make room for this new account. Poems exist as conversations that simultaneously engage the reader, the language, and the literary past. Literary theorists call this type of communication "intertextuality." I find that a useful and commonsensical notion. All literature works this way, but poems do it with special intensity and compression.

There is a special effect when an author openly acknowledges another text. It also lets the reader into your confidence as in "After a Line by Cavafy" or "In Cheever Country." Allusion is a powerful effect, though it can easily be misused. Eliot reveled in the possibilities of allusion. Look at "Marina" or, better yet, *The Waste Land*, which even includes prose notes. The poetic possibilities opened up by allusion are simply too enticing to ignore.

RLS:

Having just finished Norman Sherry's three-volume biography of Graham Greene, I was moved by his account of how this prominent Catholic novelist, in the final decades of his long life from 1904 to 1991, found that he had lost his capacity for belief, all the while doubting his unbelief, yet retained an unwavering faith. If we assume that "belief" in Greene's case refers to theological propositions, whereas "faith" denotes an underlying expectancy of assurance, would you say that his spiritual journey may be paradigmatic of other "religious" writers in the last century?

DG:

I am glad you mentioned Greene. Not only is he a writer whom I admire enormously, but he also is part of a literary tradition that has been essential to my own poetic development. Greene belonged to the great tradition of modern British and Northern Irish Catholic novelists, which includes Evelyn Waugh, Muriel Spark, Anthony Burgess, and Brian Moore. (I would like to list James Joyce, who is another personal favorite, but as an Irishman he is a slightly different case.) I have been reading and rereading these writers since I was a teenager. What gives their work such spiritual power—one might even say ferocity, especially among the comic novelists—is that they were Roman Catholics in a nation in which Catholics were a downscale and marginal minority. These writers took for granted they were addressing an audience that would treat their beliefs with condescension at best and at worst scorn. That isn't bad training for an American Catholic writer today.

RLS:

What religious characteristics in their work impressed you?

DG:

Their novels are not often religious in any conventional sense, but their books usually play out deep theological issues—often in violent and disturbing ways. (Among American Catholic writers only Flannery O'Connor matches their ferocity of vision.) It may seem odd for a poet to acknowledge prose writers as central models, but for a Catholic writer they are the best modern guides, except for Eliot and Auden. Novels such as *The Power and the Glory*, *The End of the Affair*, *A Clockwork Orange*, *Nothing Like the Sun*, *Memento Mori*, *The Prime of Miss Jean Brodie*, *Black Robe*, *A Cold Heaven*, *Decline and Fall*, and *A Handful of Dust* shaped my imagination as much as anything in contemporary American poetry. One of the many things these books taught me was to present the terrible human struggle of sin, despair, grace, and redemption—not to preach about the fruits of faith and salvation.

RLS:

What role has belief or faith played in your career as a poet? Has doubt also been essential to sustaining either one or the other?

DG:

I was raised by Italian and Mexican Catholics and attended Catholic schools for twelve years. I attended daily Mass and studied religion, church history, and theology. I learned Church Latin before Classical Latin and can still read the Latin Bible with ease. Catholicism is in my DNA—my ethnicity and my upbringing. I refuse to join the ranks of ex-Catholics, who so slavishly follow intellectual fashion as a part of upward mobility. My sympathies are with the poor and the faithful—the people who raised me. No genteel Ivy League agnostic is going to shame me into renouncing my working-class Latin identity and heritage.

All of this is only to say that every poem I have ever written reflects my Catholic worldview, especially my sense of struggle in living with my own imperfections in a fallen world. Besieged by failure and despair, tempered by humility and suffering, I hope to remain alert to God's presence in the world.

RLS:

Thank you for your candid responses throughout this interview, and all best wishes in your future endeavors.

Image Interview With Dana Gioia

(*Image*, 2012)
By Erika Koss

EK:

I once heard you say that if you could only have one art form, it would be music. Why?

DG:

I could give you reasons, but that would suggest that my response is rational. My choice of music is simply a deep emotional preference. I like the physicality of music. It is a strange art—not only profoundly beautiful, but also communal, portable, invisible, and repeatable. Its most common form is song, a universal human art that also includes poetry.

EK:

As a young man, you intended to be a composer. What led to your discovery of poetry as your vocation?

DG:

I started taking piano lessons at six, and I eventually also learned to play the clarinet and saxophone. During my teenage years, music was my ruling passion. At nineteen I went to Vienna to study music and German. But living abroad for the first time, I began to understand myself differently. I realized that I had lost the passion to be a composer. I was also out of sympathy with the dull and academic twelve-tone aesthetic then still dominant. Meanwhile, I became fascinated with poetry. I found myself spending most of my time reading and writing. Poetry chose me. I couldn't resist it.

EK:

What does it mean to be a poet in a post-literate world? Or to be a librettist in an age where opera is a struggling art form?

DG:

It doesn't bother me much. I wasn't drawn to poetry or opera because of their popularity. Their beauty and excitement drew me. Of course, I wish these arts had larger audiences, but the value of an art isn't in the size of its audience. It comes from the truth and splendor of its existence.

All that being said, let me observe that a post-print world is not a bad place for poetry. Poetry is an art that predates writing. It's essentially an auditory art. A poet today has the potential to speak directly to an audience—through public readings, radio broadcasts, recordings, and the internet. Most people don't read poetry, but they do like to hear good poems well-recited. I write mostly for the ear, and I find large and responsive audiences all over the country. The current cultural situation is tough on novelists and critics, but it isn't altogether bad for poets.

EK:

Duke Ellington objected to his music being labeled jazz, since he just considered it music. This led me to wonder if you are bothered by the term "New Formalism" being applied to your poetry.

DG:

I've never liked the term "New Formalism." It was coined in the 1980s as a criticism of young poets who wrote in rhyme, meter, and narrative. I understand the necessity of labels in a crowded and complex culture, but labels inevitably entail an element of simplification.

I've always written both in form and free verse. It seems self-evident to me that a poet should be free to use whatever techniques the poem demands. My work falls almost evenly into thirds—one third of it is in free verse, one third in rhyme and meter, and one third in meter without rhyme. I also believe that all good art is in some sense formal. Every element in a work of art should contribute to its overall expressive effect. That is what form means. Whether the form is regular or irregular, symmetrical or asymmetrical is merely a means of achieving the necessary integrity of the work.

EK:

But don't some of those early poems have a consciously oppositional spirit?

DG:

Yes, but I didn't see myself writing in opposition to free verse. Using both free and formal verse, I wrote only in opposition to the sloppy, self-indulgent, and pretentious poetry that pervaded the 1970s. I wrote against the verbose, the narcissistic, and the tone-deaf schools of poetry. Rhyme, meter, and narrative were merely techniques I explored in search of compression and expressivity.

EK:

You have frequently mentioned the impact of your mother reading poetry to you as a child. You've described her reciting Poe's "Annabel Lee" from memory. What other poems did she recite?

DG:

She loved the popular poets of her youth—writers such as Alfred, Lord Tennyson, Rudyard Kipling, Robert Service, James Whitcomb Riley, and James Greenleaf Whittier. I heard her recite chestnuts such as "Gunga Din," "Maud Muller," and "Barbara Frietchie," as well as speeches from Shakespeare's plays. The pleasure she took in these poems was contagious. She was fond of Longfellow, Byron, and Poe. Finally, she loved Ogden Nash. His "Tale of Custard the Dragon" was one of her favorites and remains one of mine. I read it to my boys, too. It is important to remember that my mother was a working-class Mexican American woman born in poverty. Despite what the professors would have us believe, average Americans once loved poetry.

EK:

I'd like to ask you about each of your earlier books of poetry before talking about your new collection. I love the title sequence of your first book, Daily Horoscope. *How did these poems begin, and how did they eventually become a sequence?*

DG:

Title tells all. I was reading the horoscope column in a newspaper when I noticed how interesting the language was—second person, future tense, intimate tone, and prophetic manner. It struck me as very much like the language of certain Modernist poems. Think of T. S. Eliot's "Preludes," Eugenio Montale's "*Ossa di seppia,*" or Hart Crane's "Voyages." Then suddenly the opening of the first poem came to me. The inspiration was so strong that over the next few weeks I filled most of a notebook with sketches. Then I had to figure out the form they should take. I could have just published a dozen or so short poems, but I felt that the poems all had a deep connection. They needed to be arranged meaningfully to suggest their affinities.

I eventually put the six best together in a sequence that addresses one protagonist through a single day from the moment in which he first wakes to a point just after he has fallen asleep at night. As I did this, the poems started to reveal things that I hadn't initially been conscious of. This is why I believe that a poet works in collaboration with the language and with the unconscious. They both have things to say that at first the poet can hardly guess. These are dense and challenging poems, but I don't think I have ever written with more intense lyricality.

An invisible mystery seems to permeate the sequence. You write that "In a moment's pause another world / reveals itself behind the ordinary." Lines like these seem to echo both fantasy and Christianity.

DG:

It was in writing this early sequence that I started to explore what has become one of my persistent themes—the sheer mystery of our existence in which the visible and invisible worlds both press upon us. In this sequence I stopped trying to sound smart—a great literary vice. I simply surrendered myself to the phenomenon and the language that I hoped would summon it. The poems are simultaneously very mundane—describing an ordinary day—and weirdly visionary. They suggest a person overwhelmed by spiritual hungers and energy who doesn't yet know how to bring them into his life. That was me in my late twenties.

EK:

Your second collection of poetry, The Gods of Winter, *is dedicated to your first son who died at four months. Did his death provoke a crisis of faith?*

DG:

No, his death simply deadened me. For several years I felt as if I existed behind a thick glass wall beyond which the rest of the world went on obliviously. I soon discovered how many other people lived in this isolated, joyless world. I met them everywhere. I had joined a secret society no one wants to enter. But I trusted my sorrow, and it eventually led me where I needed to go. I talked to other lost souls—most of them so much worse off than I was—and I learned a depth of compassion I had never experienced. I was broken, and only with immense pain and long suffering did I heal. I then discovered that I had become a different person—humbler, kinder, and more patient. Only then was I open to grace.

EK:

You have often claimed that most of your poems aren't autobiographical. But by your own account, your elegy "Planting a Sequoia" is an exception. Did you and your brothers really plant a redwood in memory of your first son with a lock of his hair and a piece of his umbilical cord wrapped in its roots—according to an old Sicilian tradition?

DG:

Yes, everything in the poem is true. I left certain things out, but poetry requires excluding some details to allow the important things to emerge more clearly. My son died suddenly a few days before Christmas. We planted the sequoia on Christmas day, but to include that particular holiday seemed too much symbolism for a poem already so burdened with emotion. My sister was around, but it seemed clearer to focus on the men since the original custom of planting a tree (usually an olive or fig tree) was a father's task. When my son died, I stopped writing for nearly a year. This was the only new poem I wrote. I carried it around in my head for months before I had the strength to write it down.

EK:

Is the tree still there?

DG:

Yes, the tree still exists. It's over sixty feet high now and perfectly proportioned. My father tended to it till the day before he died.

EK:

Your third collection, Interrogations at Noon, *begins with a poem titled "Words" and ends with the poem "Unsaid." The first poem implies that reality is greater than words. But it also affirms the importance of language "to know and remember." To me, this has always seemed one of your most distinctively Christian poems, although nothing in it is overtly religious. It seems a poem that only someone who honors the mysteries of faith could write.*

DG:

I hate to interpret my own poems. I see certain things, but they may not be what a reader sees. Any good poem leads a life independent of its author's narrow intentions. I began "Words" as an argument with postmodernism, which asserts that language is a social construction that has no exact relationship with reality (and indeed that reality itself is a cultural construction with no independent objective existence). This is, of course, pretentious posturing, a perfect example of what George Orwell calls "silly clever" thinking. No one believes that language has an exact correspondence with reality, but it is nonetheless our best tool for getting at certain truths. None of this background is essential to understanding the poem, but it was all part of my initial creative impulse. What emerged was ultimately a very Catholic sense of the relationship between language and the world.

EK:

The collection begins and ends in paradox—the power of words and the power of silence. The short final poem, "Unsaid," suggests that most of what we experience remains unexpressed in language:

Unsaid

So much of what we live goes on inside—
The diaries of grief, the tongue-tied aches

Of unacknowledged love are no less real
For having passed unsaid. What we conceal
Is always more than what we dare confide.
Think of the letters that we write our dead.

How would you answer a reader who thought that this poem contra-dicted the ideas suggested in "Words"?

DG:

Some truths can only be expressed as paradox. Existence is not a fixed and unitary state. It is fluid and dynamic, often with opposing forces pressing on us. Poems are not so much about giving answers as about unfolding questions. A good poem argues with its author and itself. I began *Interrogations at Noon* by exploring the powers and limitations of language, but I also wanted to remember how much of what we experience is never articulated but remains private. As a poet, I believe that what one leaves unsaid is often as powerful as what one says. The hard part, of course, is making the reader actually feel what is being left unsaid.

EK:

Your new book, Pity the Beautiful, *has just been published by Graywolf Press. One poem, "Prayer at Winter Solstice," consists almost entirely of paradoxical statements. This seems to be a poem that only a Californian Catholic could write.*

Prayer at Winter Solstice

Blessed is the road that keeps us homeless.
Blessed is the mountain that blocks our way.
Blessed are hunger and thirst, loneliness and all forms of desire.
Blessed is the labor that exhausts us without end.
Blessed are the night and the darkness that blinds us.
Blessed is the cold that teaches us to feel.
Blessed are the cat, the child, the cricket, and the crow.

Blessed is the hawk devouring the hare.
Blessed are the saint and the sinner who redeem each other.
Blessed are the dead calm in their perfection.
Blessed is the pain that humbles us.
Blessed is the distance that bars our joy.
Blessed is this shortest day that makes us long for light.
Blessed is the love that in losing we discover.

DG:

I'm not sure about the Californian part, but "Prayer at Winter Solstice" is probably the most Catholic poem I've ever written. It is not a poem for everyone. It offers a set of beatitudes that praise the suffering and renunciation necessary to make us spiritually alert. It celebrates the transformative and redemptive nature of suffering—one of the central spiritual truths of Christianity as well as one easily forgotten in our materialist consumer culture. It is also a poem about facing the hard realities of our existence. Our feel-good society tries to deny suffering—unless it can sell you a pill or product to banish it.

EK:

Your poem "Special Treatments Ward" has been haunting me for days, especially lines like "Risen they are healed but not made whole" or the closing line, "And vagrant sorrow cannot bless the dead." Is it too much to say that this poem began from your continuing pain at losing your first son?

DG:

This was the most difficult poem I've ever written. It began when my second son had a serious injury that required an extended stay in a children's neurological ward where nearly every other child was dying of a brain or spinal tumor. Having lost my first son, I was entirely vulnerable to the pain and confusion of the sick children

162

and their desperate parents. I began to write a poem about how unprepared everyone in the ward was for what they had to face. But the poem kept growing and changing. It took me sixteen years to finish. I didn't want to finish it. I wanted to forget it, but the poem demanded to be finished. So the poem is not about my first son or my second son, though they are both mentioned. It is about the other children who died.

EK:

Critics are not going to know what to do with "Haunted," your brilliant new narrative poem, whose very urbane narrator turns out to have a surprising identity. You have said that your poems often begin with a line or musical phrase. How did this long poem begin?

DG:

Actually, this poem began with the first two lines: "'I don't believe in ghosts,' he said. 'Such nonsense. / But years ago I actually saw one.'" As soon as I heard those two lines, the whole poem started to unfold, though it took an immense amount of work to create the narrative tone and the musical qualities I wanted. An odd thing about poetry is that when a good one comes we often realize that we have been writing it in the back of our mind for years. A single line brings it into existence almost fully formed.

"Haunted" is a ghost story that turns into a love story about a mutually destructive couple, but then at the end the reader realizes that the whole tale was really about something else entirely. The real theme is quite the opposite of what it initially seems. I wanted the poem to have the narrative drive of a short story but also rise to moments of intense lyricality. I was particularly pleased that I was able to weave humor and horror, as well as tenderness and toughness, into a continuous narrative fabric.

EK:

Flannery O'Connor said that fiction is "an incarnational art." Would you broaden this statement to include poetry?

DG:

All art is incarnational. Art doesn't consist of abstractions. It is embodied truth created for creatures with bodies. A poem doesn't communicate primarily through ideas. It expresses itself in sound, images, rhythms, and emotions. We experience poems holistically. They speak to us simultaneously through our minds, our hearts, our imaginations, and our physical bodies. They speak to us, in other words, as incarnated beings.

EK:

Some readers may be surprised to learn that your "first literary love affair" was with Edgar Rice Burroughs, especially his John Carter of Mars novels. How old were you? And what did these books spark in you?

DG:

As a boy, I loved science fiction and adventure stories. I came across Burroughs when I was about ten. I discovered an Ace paperback of *At the Earth's Core* on the bookrack of the local drugstore. Soon my friends and I bought every book by Burroughs we could find. They were just being reissued after many years. When *A Princess of Mars* and its two sequels appeared, we knew that we would never read better novels. They were full of breathless action, lofty heroics, wild fantasy, and a rather impressive vocabulary. And there was a fetching heroine — "the incomparable Dejah Thoris." What more did a bookish boy need to attain aesthetic bliss?

I eventually read forty-five of Burroughs's novels. It was the first of many literary love affairs. I remember those books as fondly as I do my first kiss. Years later I read a dozen of them aloud to my sons at bedtime. They loved them as much as I did.

EK:

You once listed Thomas Merton's The Wisdom of the Desert *as one of the most important books of your life, saying it made you realize how "spiritually starved" you were during your early years in business working at General Foods in New York. You even suggested that it eventually led you to quit your job to become a full-time writer.*

DG:

I picked up Merton's book on the desert saints quite by chance at the Gotham Book Mart in Manhattan. Its defense of the contemplative life awakened a deep hunger in my soul. Merton described how a small group of men had abandoned the sophisticated city of Alexandria in the fourth century to live and pray in the desert— renouncing material comforts and worldly ambitions to focus on their inner lives. He made a compelling case for a life dedicated to matters that the everyday world does not understand.

It's hard to describe the force with which Merton's ideas struck me. I read his many books on the contemplative life and pondered them seriously. I recognized that I was one of those odd people who need silence and solitude (even though that would have seemed absurd to anyone observing my busy and practical daily life). I knew that I needed to remake my life. Eventually I quit business and a few years later moved back to California for a quiet rural life. Merton was not entirely responsible for those changes, but he was a catalyst. And, of course, Merton was one of the writers who made me understand I had to reconnect more meaningfully with my Catholicism.

EK:

What other writers influenced you in this way?

DG:

One book that has exercised a lifelong influence on me is Saint Augustine's *City of God*, which I first read as a Stanford undergraduate. It has probably shaped my adult life more than any other book except the Gospels. Augustine helped me understand the danger of letting the institutions of power—be they business, government, or academia—in which we spend our daily lives shape our values. We need to understand what we can give to the City of Man and what we should not. I couldn't have survived my years in business as a writer had I not resisted the hunger for wealth, power, and status that pervades that world. The same was true for my years in power-mad Washington.

Another writer who helped me understand these things was the Marxist philosopher and literary critic Georg Lukács—not a name one usually sees linked with Augustine's, but he was another compelling analyst of the intellectual and moral corruptions of institutional power.

EK:

Any other writers?

DG:

So many authors have been important to me. Sometimes they spoke to a particular need I felt at a point in life. Others have been lifelong companions. Many were poets and novelists, but there were also philosophers, theologians, and thinkers. I have read and reread the works of Søren Kierkegaard, Friedrich Nietzsche, Miguel de Unamuno, Mircea Eliade, Dietrich Bonhoeffer, George Orwell, Marshall McLuhan, Jacques Maritain, and recently René Girard. I have also been particularly moved by the works of Albert Schweitzer (whom no one seems to read nowadays), especially his *The Quest of the Historical Jesus* and *The Mystery of the Kingdom of God*. I generally avoid devotional works, but for many years I always packed a copy of Thomas à Kempis's *The Imitation of Christ* in my briefcase on business trips. It helped me be a little less evil.

EK:

Since leaving the National Endowment for the Arts (and being awarded the Laetare Medal by Notre Dame), you seem to be speaking more publicly about the relationship between Catholicism and the arts. What led to this change?

DG:

When I was a public official, it was inappropriate for me to speak personally about a number of subjects. For example, while in office I never made a negative remark about any living American artist. I had my private opinions, but it was important that no one mistook those private views for public policy. I did accept numerous invitations to speak at Catholic and Christian colleges and institutions, many of which had historically felt marginalized by the NEA, but I visited them in an official capacity as cultural rather than religious institutions.

Now that I am a private citizen again, I can speak from a personal point of view. At Catholic institutions, I feel it important to remind the audiences of two facts—first, how central the arts have been historically to Catholic worship and identity; and second, how completely the church has abandoned the arts in recent times. I feel very strongly that the church needs the arts, and also that the arts need the profound traditions of spiritual awareness and practice offered by the church.

EK:

What has been the effect of this divorce between the church and the arts?

DG:

The schism has hurt both faith and the arts. The loss of a transcendent religious vision, a refined and vigorous sense of the sacred, and the ancient and powerful tradition of symbolism and allusion have impoverished the language of the arts. We see the result of this immense loss in the cynical irony, the low-cost nihilism, the sentimental spiritual pretentions, and the shallow novelty of so much contemporary art.

Please understand, I am not asking that all art be religious. That would be a disaster. I am suggesting something more subtle and complex—namely, that once you remove the religious as one of the possible modes of art, once you separate art from the long established traditions and disciplines of spirituality, you don't remove the hungers of either artists or audiences, but you satisfy them more crudely with the vague, the pretentious, and the sentimental.

EK:

What is the impact on the church?

DG:

The loss of a vital aesthetic sensibility in the church has not only impoverished worship. It has also weakened the church's identity in modern society and limited the ways in which it speaks to the world. Bad architecture, banal art, somnambulistic sermons, and mediocre music poorly performed reveal a Catholic Church that has not only cut itself off from culture, but also lost touch with its own great traditions of fostering beauty and creativity. Is it any wonder that so many artists and intellectuals have left the church?

EK:

Why has this happened? Does the Catholic Church view art as an unnecessary luxury? There has been such a rich tradition of sacred art.

168

DG:

There are many reasons. The church is rightly concerned with issues of poverty, health, education, and social justice. In the U.S., Catholicism has always been the religion of the poor, especially struggling immigrants. These are communities with huge material needs. But, to quote a relevant old phrase, "Man does not live by bread alone." Even the poorest people—perhaps especially the poor—need beauty and the transcendent. Beauty is not a luxury. It is humanity's natural response to the splendor and mystery of creation. To assume that some group doesn't need beauty is to deny their full humanity.

EK:

Do you consciously think of yourself as part of a tradition of Catholic writers?

DG:

I am a Catholic, and I am a writer. I don't think you can separate the two identities. But I have never wanted to be "a Catholic writer" in some narrow sense. Was Evelyn Waugh a Catholic writer? Was Flannery O'Connor or Muriel Spark? Well, yes and no. They were first and foremost writers who strived for imaginative power and expressive intensity. Their Catholicism entered their work along with their humor, violence, sexuality, and creative verve. The few devotional works Waugh wrote are his only dull books. His merciless early comic novels, which are Catholic only in their depiction of a hopelessly fallen world, are probably his best. Anthony Burgess's *A Clockwork Orange* is a deeply Catholic novel about free will, but it is also a brutal, dystopian science fiction novel about social collapse and political hypocrisy, all of which is narrated in an invented futuristic slang. There is something complicated going on here that cannot be simplified into faith-based writing.

I have been drawn to Catholic writers from the moment as a teenager I first read James Joyce's *Portrait of the Artist as a Young Man*. I soon began to devour the work of Waugh, Burgess, O'Connor, and Brian Moore. A little later I discovered Graham Greene and Muriel Spark. (I have read all twenty-two of her novels, most of them twice.) And let's not forget doomed and marvelous John Kennedy Toole. What these writers have in common is not simply their Catholicism, but (with the exception of Greene and Moore) that they are comic writers who luxuriate in humanity's fallen nature. None of them can be construed as a devotional writer.

EK:

I can't help notice that these are all prose writers. What about poets?

DG:

That is the problem for a Catholic poet, isn't it? There isn't a modern poetic tradition comparable to the legacy of Catholic fiction. (And I didn't even mention half of the major novelists.) The poets constitute an odd tradition, made up mostly of converts, such as Edith Sitwell, Roy Campbell, and Allen Tate. (Or temporary converts such as Robert Lowell whose flamboyant Catholicism always struck me as literary posturing.) This assemblage seems most notable for its eccentricity. I found little to sustain me there.

My poetic models were the great Modernists, such as Robert Frost, T. S. Eliot, Ezra Pound, Wallace Stevens, W. H. Auden, Paul Valéry, Rainer Maria Rilke, Eugenio Montale, and—much later—Robinson Jeffers. Of these poets, Rilke, Valéry, and Montale were raised Catholic, but none of them practiced the faith as adults. Stevens was a deathbed convert. For Catholic poets I had to go back to Dante, Shakespeare, Baudelaire, and Hofmannsthal.

There was, however, one special exception. At Harvard I studied with Robert Fitzgerald, the great translator of Homer, Virgil, and

Sophocles. He was deeply Catholic, and his teaching and literary example had a profound effect on me. One of the many things he showed me was the continuity of the Catholic imagination across European literature. (He also helped me master prosody and versification.) At Harvard I also studied with Northrop Frye, who was an ordained minister as well as professor of English. His course on myth and poetry had an enduring impact on my understanding of both literature and the Christian mythos. He was an astonishing teacher.

EK:

And what about your place in this tradition?

DG:

I don't see myself as working in an active tradition of Catholic poets because such a tradition hardly exists in contemporary American letters. I feel deep affinities with other Catholic writers, but my deepest relationships are mostly with the dead. That will make no sense to most people, but it seems quite natural to a Catholic raised on the notion of the Communion of Saints. What has sustained me has been my sense of literature as an expression of the City of God, a place one has elected to enter in contradiction to the City of Man. A poet's calling requires one to stand outside the marketplace—be it commercial or academic—and to write as well and as truthfully as one can. We don't write for the authorities—political or aesthetic. We write for the fellow citizens of our invisible city. We render unto Caesar those things that are Caesar's, but we do not render up the truth. So what is my place in this tradition? I am just another pilgrim.

EK:

Whom do you write for?

DG:

Let me begin by saying whom I don't write for. I don't write for poets or literary critics. I don't write for readers of any particular faith, politics, or aesthetic. It seems a grave danger to write only for people who share your own ideology—a kind of psychic laziness. I can't imagine writing just for Catholics. A religious poem, for instance, should speak to an atheist as much as a believer. It might speak differently perhaps, but it needs to transcend any system of belief and touch some common humanity. Maybe "transcend" is the wrong word. "Exceed" might be better. John Donne's "divine" poems have such an excess of meaning that their appeal isn't limited to Anglicans. The same is true of Dante, Hopkins, Eliot, Auden, or Dylan Thomas.

EK:

Who then is your audience?

DG:

I write for other human beings who both resemble me and differ from me in ways I can't predict. I hope for readers who are alert and intelligent, though not necessarily learned. I speak to deeply felt experience rather than to higher education, though I do usually conceal a few jokes that only the erudite will catch. I still believe in what Samuel Johnson called "the common reader," who is not an unintelligent reader but one open to pleasure and surprise. I was raised among the working poor, and I know that intelligence and creativity are found in every class and race and region. A poet should entice rather than exclude.

EK:

Over the years you have been put in many categories. You've been called a New Formalist poet, a California poet. Why do you think your identity as a Catholic poet has been overlooked until quite recently?

DG:

Most readers are very literal. They focus mostly on subject matter. Since I didn't write poems about the crucifixion or the Virgin Mary, it never occurred to them that I was a Catholic poet. What makes my poetry Catholic is the worldview, the sacramental use of symbols, the redemptive role of suffering, the interpenetration of the sacred and the mundane, and—crucially perhaps—the conviction that truth and beauty are interdependent. I'm not drawn to the stage business of Catholicism—its pomp and circumstance. I write from the daily particulars of real life. You shouldn't have to visit the Vatican to sense the divine. It is everywhere if you know how to look.

EK:

In a 2003 article in Commonweal *you said, "American intellectual culture remains unconsciously anti-Catholic." Do you still regard this to be true?*

DG:

No. American intellectual culture has now become *consciously* anti-Catholic. I now regularly read the most overtly bigoted things in the press, things that no one would say about any other group. At present it seems *de rigeur* to hate Catholics as impediments to secular progress. Robespierre felt the same way during the French Revolution. I guess we should feel grateful that our intellectual pundits don't own guillotines.

EK:

How does the Catholic vision differ from other traditions of Christianity?

DG:

To answer that question would require a shelf of books. There are so many Christian traditions. But let me mention one aspect of Catholicism that affects the writer. All Christian denominations believe in original sin and humanity's fallen nature, but Catholicism emphasizes the slow and difficult nature of the personal struggle toward salvation. The notion of suddenly being "saved" feels alien to Catholics. We see life as a pilgrimage in which each step forward can easily be followed by a fall backward from grace. For that reason the great Catholic writers characteristically write about the experience of sinners rather than saints, often people of great spiritual capacity who have lost their way. O'Connor's mass murderer the Misfit is one example. Another is Greene's nameless whiskey priest.

EK:

Isn't this emphasis on the dark side of humanity mostly a modern aspect of Catholic literature?

DG:

Think of the greatest Catholic poem ever written, Dante's *Commedia*, which was finished around 1320. Where does it begin? In the dark wood of despair where a lost sinner must confront the terrifying embodiments of his own sins. How does the poet start his transformative journey toward grace? He descends into the darkness of hell to experience the nature of evil. That spiritual premise is profoundly Catholic. This emphasis on human weakness, spiritual failure, and evil allows the writer to explore the full range of human experience. The great theme of Catholic imaginative literature is the violent and painful struggle for redemption in a fallen world.

I am devoted to gentle books such as the *Fioretti* of Saint Francis of Assisi, but they lack the dramatic intensity of *The Power and the Glory* or "A Good Man Is Hard to Find." Catholic literature seldom feels the need to be uplifting or devotional. Instead it depicts the difficult road to salvation in a fallen world. François Mauriac's harrowing novel *Nest of Vipers* has only one secondary character who is not morally contemptible, but it profoundly explores the redemptive nature of love. These writers present life in its rich and contradictory complexity while viewing it from the perspectives of faith. That is a potent combination. By comparison, American Protestant writing has often tried to present good people doing good things. Occasionally a masterpiece such as Marilynne Robinson's *Gilead* appears, but it is a harder task to realize.

EK:

Except for Dante, you've talked about fiction. What about Catholic poetry?

DG:

Dante is not an exception. The great Catholic poets tend to wrestle with the darker spiritual emotions—guilt, doubt, and despair. For every great joyous poem Gerard Manley Hopkins wrote, there is a corresponding dark one. That's why I regard Baudelaire a central figure in Catholic poetry. He saw himself as a man who was damned by his own sins. All he had left at a certain point was to revel in his own damnation. Catholic poetry ponders the possibility of damnation. But while it rejects the sort of sentimentality that vitiates so much religious poetry, it also opens itself to the immanence of grace. One sees this in the best Catholic poetry—in Hopkins, for instance, or Mario Luzi, the Italian Modernist whom I consider the greatest Catholic poet of the twentieth century. Not the easiest, by any means, but a religious poet of international stature. He is hardly read in America and never—in my experience—by Catholics.

EK:

After avoiding academic employment for years, you have just accepted a half-time position at the University of Southern California as the first Judge Widney Professor of Poetry and Public Culture. What was your first semester like at USC?

DG:

I like USC. It has the strongest collection of arts programs of any university in the country, and it is full of abundantly creative people. The place is also strikingly optimistic and confident about the future—a rare thing at the moment for a university. It was also wonderful to be back in my old hometown.

I taught two courses—an undergraduate survey of modern American poetry and a graduate seminar on "Words and Music" at USC's Thornton School of Music. The seminar explored material that lies outside the conventional scope of musical study—the relationship between poetry and music in opera, song, worship, and theater. It was a challenge to put the material together in a coherent form, especially since my students were singers, composers, and instrumentalists who mostly lacked any literary education. I enjoyed exploring the conjunction of the two arts.

EK:

What are your plans for the future?

DG:

After eight years in Washington, I want a quieter life. I want to return to writing poetry and essays. I will be teaching each fall at USC, and that will be my public life, which will be active and engaged. But the rest of the year I hope to hide in Sonoma County. I like to divide the day into writing and manual labor. I have twenty hilly acres of oaks, redwoods, and madrones, and there is always work to do. I'm trying to restore the landscape to its natural state and protect the native species. No one really cares about this goal but me. My neighbors think I should tear out the trees and plant grapes. But I prefer the place the way God landscaped it.

III

The Epistle of Paul to the Philippians

A poet writing about the New Testament faces two kinds of intimidation. First comes the challenge of biblical scholarship. Probably no other area of human study has generated so much research, commentary, and criticism as the Bible. The New Testament alone has inspired two thousand years of continuous explication across innumerable languages, living and dead. The mass of writing on the subject is not merely unmanageable but unthinkably vast. (In comparison with Paul and the Evangelists, Shakespeare is a young playwright getting his first notices.) When a theologian can spend a lifetime without mastering the heritage of Christian Scripture, what is the non-specialist to do? The learned commentators cannot agree even on fundamental issues of authorship, chronology, historical fidelity, textual accuracy, and translation—not to mention interpretation.

The second problem facing a poet is one of religious belief—not only his or her own credo but those of each possible audience. In the West no texts are more charged with moral, spiritual, and even political significance than the books of the New Testament. Most readers bring a lifetime of preconceptions to each major text and topic. A cleric writing to fellow members of a particular sect (be it Roman Catholic, Greek Orthodox, or Southern Baptist) can assume a common set of beliefs. But a writer trying to address a general audience knows there will be disagreements about basic issues no matter what one chooses to say. For many readers every passage of the New Testament is the living word of God, infallibly speaking the literal truth to humankind. For others it is a magnificent account of tribal myths no different from the Hindu *Bhagavad-Gita* or the Egyptian *Book of the Dead*. And for still others—including most American intellectuals—it is an influential moral document in which great truths are unfortunately tangled up with discredited supernatural legend.

Faced with these obstacles, most literary writers have stopped discussing Scripture. Their reticence has left the subject mostly to specialists. As a result, both American letters and religion have been the poorer. Moreover, as literary and religious writing have divided, so have their audiences. Today few literary readers know the Bible well. The little they have read—perhaps the Book of Job—was usually last encountered in a college survey course. Secular intellectuals now know the Bible mainly from visual sources, most notably Renaissance painting. The divorce between Christianity and high culture has progressed so far that even sophisticated readers now have difficulty understanding basic biblical texts. Buttressed neither by familiarity nor by faith, they lack the intellectual and historical frames of reference to interpret them with even minimal accuracy. Such readers may understand the words of a scriptural passage but often miss the cultural context that gives it meaning.

The obstacles to understanding are particularly daunting in the epistles of Saint Paul. These central Christian documents promise the accessibility and clarity of personal letters, but to most modern readers their contexts seem obscure, their purposes clouded, and their structures elusive. Paul's letters lack the narrative appeal of the Gospels and the Acts of the Apostles, where the story pulls the reader along. Nor do the epistles have the poetic splendor and enticing mystery of Revelation (which Catholics used to call by the more exciting title, The Apocalypse). Everyone loves a puzzle, especially one that promises to explain the end of the world. With Revelation, the reader expects to be mystified initially, and John of Patmos does not disappoint with his eschatological *roman à clef*. Among the books of the New Testament, only the epistles fail to satisfy the generic expectations they raise.

Paul of Tarsus himself is also a difficult figure for modern readers. While he ranks as the most important personality in early Christianity (after, of course, Jesus, who even to non-believers occupies a special status), Paul remains very much a man of his distant time and place. Energetic, argumentative, intellectual, he lacks the simple human touch that Jesus exhibits in the Gospels. Jesus taught by parable and proverb. Paul instructed by abstraction and explanation. One cannot dispute that Paul's method was effective. More than any other individual, he built the institutional enterprise of Christianity by codifying Jesus's teaching into a systematic set of principles—a new covenant designed to replace the Hebrew original. But one must also recognize that the practical and ideological nature of Paul's first-century mission now makes his writing less accessible. While Jesus's sermons still seem fresh and immediate after two thousand years, Paul's homilies require explanation and amplification.

Amplification and explanation have been endlessly forthcoming. Commentary began at Paul's death and has never stopped. Some commentaries even took the form of pious imitations. While the Epistle to the Philippians is genuinely the Apostle's work, as many as half of the other epistles bearing his name may have been written by his followers. These pseudo-Pauline letters, in which early disciples probably took genuine fragments and elaborated them into fictive letters, were the earliest responses to Paul's work. Likewise, much subsequent Christian theology from St. Augustine to Karl Barth, has taken the form of creative reinterpretation of his ideas. Writers often wrestle with their most powerful predecessors to win intellectual independence. For ambitious theologians, the figure waiting in the ring has most often been Paul the tentmaker.

If imaginative writers like me have anything to add to the understanding of Paul, it is probably mostly our innocence and humanity. We might know the epistles, but not so well that we forget how foreign and confusing they seem to new readers. We realize that the critic's job, like the artist's, is one of translation—in Paul's case not simply from Greek into English but from an ancient mind to a modern one. Part of that translation derives from scholarship. We are of no use there. But the other part comes from imagination—not in its everyday sense of constructing fictions but in its higher sense of the intuitive discovery of reality. Perhaps the major difference between the artist and the scholar is in the role of the imagination. Scholars use imagination as a secondary faculty, always in service to the known facts. For the poet or novelist, the imagination is primary. It employs facts as a point of departure, not into mere fantasy but toward clarifying speculation. Likewise, the artist prizes the concrete and human detail and shies away from the theoretical and abstract. A poet may miss the theological implications in a phrase of Paul's but will instinctively catch the psychological state or emotional tone. By virtue of training, a literary artist is alert to the human side of a text.

I will examine Paul's Epistle to the Philippians, therefore, in the best way I can—as a poet. I write knowing my impossible position as middleman between the erudite scholar and general reader. But today any artist writing about any classic, sacred or secular, faces the same problem. How does one discuss a work about which everything has been said while no one outside the classroom was listening? The answer does not come from ignoring scholarship. Honest inquiry begins in knowledge. But the artist must resist letting scholarship dictate the issues to be addressed. One must try to engage the work itself and discuss only what frankly interests, annoys, or puzzles one about it.

For me, the most remarkable feature of the Epistle to the Philippians is its tangible humanity. Although ideas from the letter have been enormously influential, it constitutes no theological treatise. Paul's ideas develop less through sustained argument than by emotional association. The form of the epistle seems less intellectual than dramatic. One must consider Paul's personal situation at the time of its composition and his relationship with the church members he addresses. Tracing the implied narrative is the best way to approach this difficult epistle.

Let me begin, however, by acknowledging how difficult it is for the first-time reader to piece together the human story of Philippians. The letter is short, only 104 verses, but they are packed with information. The structure is subjective and digressive. There is no single line of thought or narrative. Even the circumstances that occasioned the letter are initially hard to unravel. Paul's thanks for the Philippians' assistance occurs so late in the epistle that it initially seems like an afterthought. (This peculiarity has led some scholars to suggest that the surviving text is actually a composite of several letters written by Paul at different times.) Finally, the epistle deals with several issues, such as ritual circumcision, that make little sense to the contemporary reader untutored in early Christian ideological debate.

Despite its casual organization, the first-time reader can immediately feel the emotional intensity of this extraordinary epistle. Written when Paul, an old man worn out by years of travel and persecution, waited in Roman custody under the threat of execution, the epistle achieves a spiritual clarity of the most intimate kind. Paul talks as much about his own struggle for salvation as about the Philippians' situation. In a moment of uncharacteristic weakness, he even confesses that he would prefer to join Christ in death than to persevere in life against so many obstacles:

> For me to live is Christ, and to die is gain.
> But if I live in the flesh, this is the fruit of my labor: yet what I shall choose I wot not.
> For I am in a strait betwixt two, having a desire to depart, and to be with Christ: which is far better:
> Nevertheless to abide in the flesh is more needful for you.
>
> (1:21-24)

Reading Paul's intimate words, one naturally wonders who the people were he addressed. How did they come to have such a candid and affectionate relationship with the formidable apostle? In biblical studies such questions are usually impossible to answer. In the case of Philippians, however, we have Paul's earlier relationship with the Macedonian church documented elsewhere in the New Testament. In his Acts of the Apostles, Luke provides an eyewitness account of Paul's first visit to Philippi because the evangelist accompanied him on the journey. Not only is Luke's story an illuminating account of early Christian missionary work; it also explains the privileged position the church at Philippi occupied in Paul's heart.

Luke tells how, early in his missionary career, Paul had preached in Palestine and Asia Minor. Each time he turned to go eastward into Asia, the Holy Spirit had stopped him. Finally one night Paul, Timothy, Silas, and Luke were in Troas, at the tip of Asia Minor, pointing toward Greece. That night Paul had a vision in which a man appeared and said, "Come over into Macedonia and help us." The four men sailed to Macedonia and went directly to Philippi, the region's principal city, which was located on the main road between Rome and Asia Minor. Their arrival in Philippi marked the first Christian mission to the West. The congregation they founded became the first Christian church in Europe.

The Jewish community in Philippi was too small to maintain a synagogue, so the faithful gathered on a riverbank outside the city walls. Paul preached there and made a convert, a well-to-do fabric dyer named Lydia, the first European Christian on record. She took the apostle and his company into her home. Paul continued preaching in the city until a curious event led him into legal trouble. A possessed slave girl, who had earned her masters considerable money with her gift of prophecy, started following Paul's company, crying, "These men are the servants of the most high God, which show unto us the way of salvation." (In the New Testament the demonically possessed quickly recognize the sanctity of Christ and his apostles, even if the normal folk do not.) Paul exorcised the slave, to the annoyance of her masters, since she now lost her profitable ability. They brought criminal charges against Paul and Silas, who were beaten, put into stocks, and incarcerated.

Locked in an inner dungeon, Paul and Silas prayed and sang hymns until midnight, when, according to Luke, a miraculous earthquake opened all the prison doors and shook off their chains. The jailer, alarmed that his charges had escaped, was about to take his own life. Then Paul called out from his dark cell that none of the prisoners had left. The jailer asked to be converted and took the Christians into his own home. The next day the local magistrates, who now feared both Paul's supernatural power and his Roman citizenship (which legally protected him from the peremptory beating they had inflicted), set the missionaries free with the request to leave the city. Once liberated, Paul and his companions briefly visited the house of Lydia and then departed.

Luke's account of Paul's mission to Philippi raises an inescapable issue for any modern reader—namely, the presence of miracles. In this brief episode one finds six supernatural events: the intervention of the Holy Spirit, the prophetic apparition in Paul's vision, the demonic possession, the possessed girl's ability to tell fortunes, the publicly acknowledged exorcism, and the wondrous earthquake. Luke narrates these events as matters of fact. Since the Enlightenment biblical scholars have fretted over such miraculous episodes in the New Testament. Commentators often try to explain them as literary symbols, unreliable hearsay uncritically accepted by New Testament authors, or later textual additions. In Acts, however, Luke appears to offer an eyewitness account of the events at Philippi, and throughout the authentic Pauline Epistles Paul repeatedly alludes to similar wonders done in Christ's name. They are not incidental to the larger narrative.

Even if one discounts the miracles reported in the Pauline Epistles, a more fundamental problem remains. Paul claims that he gained his knowledge of the Christian gospel not from the man Jesus—whom Paul never saw in the flesh—nor even from the other apostles, but from a miraculous vision of the risen Christ on the road to Damascus. Luke unreservedly accepts the claim. There can be no textual ambiguity here. As Paul himself makes clear in both First Corinthians and Galatians (1:11-12), he does not preach a gospel "given to him by man but directly by the revelation of Jesus Christ."

Contemporary scholars may lament Paul's dependence on supernatural evidence to assert the verity of the Christian faith. They may wish he practiced a more modern theology emphasizing the ethical nature of Christ's gospel. But the basic problem remains. Paul believed in Christ's divinity because he was given direct physical proof—not only outside Damascus but repeatedly elsewhere by divine guidance and supernatural intervention. What made Christ important for him was not merely Jesus's redemptive moral vision. Paul claimed direct knowledge that Jesus rose from the dead, ascended into heaven, and soon would return to judge all humanity. Moreover, he believed that Christ would return within the lifetime of newly converted church members. As he says in Philippians 4:5, "The Lord is at hand." There was nothing abstract at the center of Paul's "gospel." In his own eyes, he was a passionate realist. Surely ancient readers would have understood the extraordinary nature of Paul's assertions just as clearly as modern readers do. If Paul was inaccurate in reporting such miracles, how can one trust his veracity or rationality in any other matter? The reader has no choice but to view Paul as either a psychotic or a saint.

I have no desire to dictate the reader's choice between the alternative interpretations of Paul. I insist only that the issue cannot be avoided. Scholarship, however masterful, will resolve nothing. Enough authentic letters by Paul have survived to make his central claims of direct divine guidance unambiguous. The diagnosis one makes of Paul's reliability will affect the reading of every book in the New Testament, and this verdict ultimately depends on one's assumptions about Christ's divinity. In rational terms, the Incarnation is impossible. A Christian must endorse it against both logic and common sense. Christian faith, as Tertullian asserted, is based on an absurd proposition: *Certum est quia impossibile* ("It is certain because impossible"). If one accepts Christianity, it must be done, as Paul tells the Philippians, "in fear and trembling." Accepting Christ annihilates one's previous sense of reality.

At the end of Flannery O'Connor's chilling story "A Good Man Is Hard to Find," there is a conversation between a murderer nicknamed The Misfit and an old woman. The Misfit's gang has just murdered her family, and he is about to kill her. She mumbles "Jesus, Jesus" out of fear, and he unexpectedly begins to discuss Christianity with her in coldly rational terms that Paul would have understood:

> "Jesus was the only One that ever raised the dead," The Misfit continued, "and He shouldn't have done it. He thown

everything off balance. If He did what He said, then it's nothing for you to do but thow away everything and follow Him, and if He didn't, then it's nothing for you to do but enjoy the few minutes you got left the best way you can. . . ."

Paul said nearly the same thing, echoing Ecclesiastes, in 1 Corinthians 1:32: "What advantageth it me, if the dead rise not? Let us eat and drink, for tomorrow we die."

Writing to the Philippians, Paul feels no need to argue forcefully about the reality of the central Christian message. He takes the congregation's faith for granted. The church he founded in Macedonia has remained strong and loyal. The congregation is sober and devout. They have supported Paul financially on his missions in Thessalonica, Corinth, and Rome. His epistle is an expression of gratitude to people who had played an important part in his life. Writing from prison, Paul thanks them in particular for sending him both money and a helper. He tells the Philippians that Epaphroditus, the assistant they sent, has been seriously ill and now wants to return home. The epistle was presumably carried by Epaphroditus to Philippi, where it was read and preserved.

The short epistle is relaxed and conversational, since Paul is writing old friends. Because Paul strays from one topic to another, some scholars maintain that the canonic text is a composite of several separate letters sent to the fledgling church. Yet this amiable epistle is no more digressive than most long letters. Paul is full of news and advice. To focus on the epistle's structural deficiencies is to miss a more noteworthy quality—its gentle intimacy—which makes it unique among Paul's epistles.

A particular beauty of Paul's letter to the Philippians is the tangible affection and trust the apostle felt for the recipients. Philippians is not only Paul's warmest surviving epistle, it is also the most joyful. As many commentators have noted, the words for "joy" and "rejoice" appear twenty-two times in a relatively short letter. Paul's tone is friendly and intimate rather than defensive or excited. For once he

187

relaxed his frequently argumentative manner. Unlike the Galatians or Corinthians, the Macedonian church gives him no cause for outburst and admonition. Of course, complete serenity is too much to expect from Paul. He has one explosive moment in the epistle's third chapter, where he warns of the danger from the Judaizers, who demanded circumcision for male converts. But even this brief harangue seems friendly by Pauline standards. The Philippians would probably have worried about their old teacher's health had he not gotten his temper up at least once.

The opening verses of Philippians highlight its special qualities. Paul begins in his customary manner by identifying himself and Timothy as well as his recipients in Philippi. But then the letter takes an unusually emotional turn as Paul admits his special affection for the members of this church. He confesses he cannot remember them without thanking God for the joy their exemplary fellowship brings him. He also confides how much he misses their company. Paul frequently wrote to resolve problems in local churches, but to the Philippians he writes to praise and exhort them. He does not ask the congregation to change its behavior, only to continue it.

The heart of the epistle is the second chapter, which outlines the goals of Christian life and sets Christ as the model for humility and obedience to God. The thirty verses of this chapter are one of the central texts of Christianity. The passage has inspired theologians from Augustine to the present. Paul begins the chapter with a series of conditional statements beginning with "if." As any student of Paul's rhetoric knows, when the apostle begins a statement with "if," then rhapsodic affirmation will usually follow:

> If there be therefore any consolation in Christ, if any comfort of
>   love, if any fellowship of the Spirit, if any bowels and mercies,
> Fulfil ye my joy, that ye be likeminded, having the same love, being
>   of one accord, of one mind.
> Let nothing be done through strife or vainglory; but in lowliness
>   of mind let each esteem other better than themselves.
>
> (2:1-3)

At the center of this crucial chapter is a magnificent poem that constitutes the spiritual and literary focus of the epistle. Six verses (2:6-11) had long been recognized as the most elevated and mysterious part of Paul's epistle. But the passage did not seem characteristic of Paul's prose style. It was not until 1928 that the German scholar Ernst Lohmeyer demonstrated that the oddly worded passage generally fell into a metrical rhythm in the original Greek. Though skillfully woven into the prose of Paul's letter, the passage is poetic. The six lines form a hymn to Christ's incarnation and death. Paul introduces the passage by reminding the Philippians to imitate Christ. Then he switches into verse:

> Being in the form of God,
> He considered it not a thing to be seized
> To be equal with God;
>
> But emptied Himself
> By taking the form of a slave,
> Coming in human likeness.
>
> And appearing on earth as Man,
> He humbled Himself,
> Becoming obedient unto death
>
> (Indeed, death on a cross)
>
> Wherefore God exalted Him
> And bestowed on Him the name
> That is above every name:
>
> That in the name of Jesus
> Every knee should bow
> In heaven, on earth, and under the earth,
>
> And every tongue confess:
> "Jesus Christ is Lord;"
> To the glory of God the Father.
>
> (Translated by Ralph A. Martin)

189

This hymn may be the earliest surviving Christian poem. No one knows whether Paul himself wrote the hymn or simply quoted it from early liturgy. Its authorship has become the subject of scholarly debate. Its original source, however, matters little to the average reader. Who can doubt that the author of the thirteenth chapter of First Corinthians ("Though I speak with the tongues of men and of angels . . . ") was capable of composing sublime poetry? If Paul did not author the Christological hymn, there is no doubt that he quoted it with total approval. What matters is the spiritual vision of the hymn. It transforms the human virtues Paul celebrates earlier into the divine values embodied by Christ's incarnation.

The hymn at the center of Philippians articulates the radical change in values offered by Christianity. Jesus presented his followers with a new form of divinity, one based not on power and pride but on self-abasement and compassion. Paul glorified the virtues of humility, charity, and obedience. The essential Christian qualities were as difficult for his contemporaries to cultivate as for us today. Paul knew the commandment to esteem others more than one's own self went against human nature, but he believed the aspiring Christian would be aided by God. As Paul wrote in a passage that Søren Kierkegaard would later take to heart: "Work out your own salvation with fear and trembling. For it is God which worketh in you both to will and to do his good pleasure" (2:12-13). Paul also testifies that God will reward the faithful for their humility, charity, and obedience.

Now comes the most intimate and vulnerable moment in the letter. The apostle asks the Philippians to strive for spiritual perfection despite the evil around them, so that their example will prove before God that his own life has not been spent in vain:

> Do all things without murmurings and disputings:
> That ye may be blameless and harmless, the sons of God, without
>   rebuke, in the midst of a crooked and perverse nation, among
>   whom ye shine as lights in the world;

Holding forth the word of life; that I may rejoice in the day of
Christ, that I have not run in vain, neither labored in vain.

(2:14-16)

What makes Paul's hope for the church's fidelity especially moving
is that he wrote the Philippians from prison. The letter probably was
sent from Rome, where he awaited trial for disturbing the peace in
Jerusalem. This assumption places the composition of Philippians
late in Paul's career. Consequently, Philippians could be Paul's last
surviving letter.

Wherever he was imprisoned, Paul made the general circumstances
of his situation clear to his friends at Philippi. He was in Roman custody waiting for a judicial decision from the emperor which would
either set him free or condemn him to death. The letter's serenity
demonstrates the Apostle's capacity for joy in the face of martyrdom.
There are no complaints, only resolution. If he lives, he knows, he
will continue to preach the gospel. If he dies, he will join Christ.
Either way, he states, "Christ will be magnified in my body, whether
it be by life or death." Paul may be in Roman custody, but his mind
refuses to be fettered by Caesar's laws.

The Epistle to the Philippians occupies a significant place in the
tradition of prison literature. The Pauline letters are the earliest
Christian works in this classical tradition. Along with the dialogues
Plato wrote depicting Socrates under the death sentence (the
Apology, *Crito*, and *Phaedo*), the Pauline prison epistles (Philippians,
Philemon, and Colossians) created the genre that would provide
models for writers from Boethius through Dostoevsky, Wilde,
Gramsci, Bonhoeffer, and Mandela. Philippians sets the visionary
tone of this tradition. Paul's letter also reveals the spiritual paradoxes
that later writers would adopt. If one is trapped in finite space, one
can nonetheless contemplate infinite things. If one must face
mortality, one can meditate on eternity. If one is held in the worst
place society offers, one can dream of the just city.

Augustine's City of God began in Paul's cell. The word can free the spirit, if not the body. The quality of the vision, however, is only as good as the moral character that produces it. Prison has also occasioned the diseased writings of de Sade and Hitler. But for some the adversity of imprisonment set the ultimate spiritual challenge which provoked their greatest work.

If Paul's Epistle to the Philippians is indeed his final work, then its personal testament reveals the Apostle's continued spiritual growth of his last years. An exhausted old man facing death, he achieved a psychological independence from his physical circumstances by embracing the Christian ideal of redemptive suffering. The worse his situation became the greater his sense of freedom. The toughness of his earlier public self softened into an unguarded gentleness and compassion. His often-explosive temper relaxed into gratitude and joy. Living his difficult principles, he attained the security he promised his friends at Philippi, "the peace of God which passeth all understanding."

According to Catholic tradition, Paul was condemned to death by the authorities in Rome. He was taken to the place now called Tre Fontane and beheaded. His body was buried where the Basilica of Saint Paul Outside-the-Walls now stands. His head was preserved and eventually placed at the center of the Archbasilica of St. John Lateran, the first Christian Church in Rome, which is now the ecclesiastical seat of the Pope and the Mother Church of Roman Catholicism. The two great basilicas still stand as the Apostle's monuments. Paul's greatest memorial, however, remains the church he founded on the riverbank outside Philippi, which inaugurated Western Christianity. If ever a monument proved more durable than bronze or loftier than the pyramids, it was that loyal congregation.

To Witness Truth Uncompromised:
Modern Martyrs

The twentieth century has reminded Christians that the history of the faith is inextricably bound with the sacrifices of its martyrs. Their example is not incidental to the Church's identity. Their deaths testify to the faith's continuing authenticity. Martyrs are not historical relics of Christianity's origins, early believers risking death to follow Christ's teachings. They represent the perpetual challenge of believers to witness their faith in a fallen world. Even in the twentieth century, most died anonymously. The names that survive constitute a litany of the vast violence that has marked the modern age.

To late-nineteenth-century Western Christians, martyrdom had become an exotic concept—a tragic event located either in the past or on the fringes of colonial empires. The missionary or native killed in a foreign persecution represented a remote risk faced by a relatively small number of believers. Martyrdom was something that occurred *elsewhere*. Within the geographical entity once called Christendom, such heroic witnessing seemed unlikely to reoccur. The Victorian mind believed earnestly in moral progress. The evidence of ethical evolution was everywhere—the abolition of slavery, universal education, national self-determination, trade unions, civil liberties, religious tolerance, all matched by myriad scientific and medical advances. Enlightened Christians could not resist being swept up in the positivistic fervor. The emergence of a just and tolerant Christian civilization, at least in Europe and North America, seemed not merely possible but historically inevitable.

The tragic events of the twentieth century demonstrated that moral progress is neither linear nor inevitable. The dialectic of history may push forward, but progress is painful, precarious, and intermittent. No sooner has some form of tyranny been banished than it reemerges in a new and equally pernicious form. The most frightening lesson of the century was how easily good impulses turn toward evil ends. The nationalistic hunger for self-determination among nineteenth-century Germans and Italians became the militaristic fascism of the 1930s. The utopian egalitarianism of Russian progressives soon fostered the Great Terror, the Ukrainian Famine, and the gulags. Cambodia's desire to transcend colonialism created Pol Pot and his re-education centers. These are lessons no one wanted to learn; they are forgotten at mortal risk. Yet these bitter episodes, so uncomfortable to sunny and sentimental middle-class Christianity, are being forgotten. The idea of martyrdom is again considered remote and abstract.

The suffering of others is easy to bear. Most Western Christians are resigned to religious intolerance in other places. They show little surprise that persecution and martyrdom follow Christians in non-Christian societies. Recent religious persecution in Egypt, China, Myanmar, Syria, Sri Lanka, Uganda, and Pakistan appear almost inevitable because Christians are minorities in those nations. Religious animosities merge with local politics in most persecutions. To established local power, Christianity often seems a threatening, foreign importation. (Two millennia ago Roman civil authorities considered it a threatening, Eastern importation.) The rights and safety of religious minorities always remain uncertain in times of political and social upheaval.

The modern persecution of Christians in Western nations such as Germany, Russia, Mexico, and, Colombia as well as the murderous struggle between Christian factions in Northern Ireland and Rwanda suggest something more unsettling. Perhaps true professing Christians are always a minority everywhere, even in Christian societies. The example of professing Christians always runs the risk of disturbing political authorities. Contemporary Christians need to understand this troubling issue, and the best place to begin is the example of modern martyrs—the believers of our own age who were forced to choose death rather than spiritual betrayal.

Sanctity is no safeguard against oblivion. Contemporary culture lives so completely in the present tense, especially in America, that it has little time for the past. One necessary task of intellectuals is to remember and study the past. Christians face the same challenge. The early church recognized the importance of martyrs by painstakingly preserving their names and stories. But how can one memorialize the myriad Christians who have died for their faith in the last century? The numbers run into the millions. How many modern martyrs went to their deaths unrecorded—in gulags, concentration camps, "reeducation" centers, prison yards, or empty fields? Their testimony is lost. It is important, therefore, that Christian intellectuals preserve the memory of martyrs whose persecution was chronicled. Their examples constitute an essential part of modern Christianity. Their struggles demonstrate the enduring moral strength generated by even a few individuals resisting evil. Would it be too much to hope that in the twenty-first century Maximilian Kolbe, Dietrich Bonhoeffer, Oscar Romero, and Edith Stein become as well-known as Hitler's generals?

Who were the modern martyrs? What crimes earned them death? Bonhoeffer, Kolbe, Romero, and Stein are widely known, but it is worthwhile to list a few of their less-known contemporaries. Bernhard Lichtenberg was the provost of the Berlin cathedral. When he protested the government execution of the insane, he was arrested and died in transit to Dachau. Franz Jagerstater was an Austrian peasant and father of three small children. Inspired by Pius XI's 1937 anti-Nazi encyclical, which condemned Hitler's racism and religious intolerance, Jagerstater refused military service in the German army. He was arrested and beheaded. Father Franz Reinisch refused to swear an oath of allegiance to Hitler and was executed. Heinz Bello, a medical student, expressed his dissatisfaction with German militarism. During a fire watch, he pointed to a cross that had been left in a barracks, saying, "So long as there is a God in Heaven, there is a limit to what can happen on earth." He was machine-gunned in Berlin's Tegel prison. His last words were *Omnia ad maiorem Dei gloriam!* ("All for the greater glory of God").

The capital crime of these people was not active political resistance (though other Christians chose that path); their offense was moral dissent. They refused complicity in evil deeds. They did not seek death, though they faced it heroically. During his trial Bello declined the opportunity to escape to Switzerland. At his sentencing he refused another chance to flee. He accepted death as the cost of witnessing.

These four men were only a few of the martyrs from one nation, the now dismantled German Reich. What of the multitudes who died elsewhere? Some we know by name. In 1927 Miguel Pro, a young Mexican Jesuit, was executed under false charges of political conspiracy by the anticlerical government of Mexico. Chinese missionary Lizzie Atwater was pregnant with her first child when she was hacked to death in the Boxer Rebellion. In 1928 Manche Mosemola of South Africa was killed by her own parents because the teenager wanted to be baptized in the Anglican Communion. Most modern martyrs, however, remain both nameless and numberless.

No one knows how many Armenian Christians were murdered by the Turks during the genocide unleashed from 1915 to 1917, an enormity still officially denied by Turkey. Was it one million? One and a half million? When every member of a family or every inhabitant of a village is slaughtered, who can keep count? How many thousands died in Uganda, Cambodia, Ethiopia, China, Mexico, and Zaire? How many millions in the Soviet Union? Modern martyrology consists of imponderables. While acknowledging how much remains unrecorded, one can begin with what is known. There will be no shortage of verifiable candidates. Examining the martyrs of the present age, however, is difficult enough because the political storms to which they fell prey are sometimes still raging.

Discussions of modern martyrs often tumble uncontrollably into political debates. Critics on both ends of the political spectrum habitually dismiss martyrs of opposing ideological persuasions. An abomination is less offensive when it happens to one's opponents. A leftist might characterize a turn-of-the-century missionary killed in China as a hapless victim of imperialism, just as a rightist might claim that an activist Latin American priest died for political reasons. Such narrowly secular interpretations not only trivialize the Christian idea of martyrdom; they also misunderstand how martyrdom inevitably brings religious and political worldviews into conflict.

Religious persecution usually contains a political element. The paradigm of Christian martyrdom is the individual who refuses to bend his or her faith to the demands of political authority. The martyr represents the heroic integrity of the conscientious individual resisting the moral compromises that the average citizen finds expedient. Although the martyr's resistance is fundamentally spiritual, an absolutist state will view it in political terms. To such secular authority, all dissent is political. To suggest that anyone but Caesar decides what must be rendered to the state is sedition.

The clash between sacred and secular duty goes back to the origins of Christianity. As Kenneth Woodward observes in *Making Saints*, "Jesus himself was persecuted for attacking the Temple authorities," and early Christian persecution originated in refusals to worship the emperor as divine or participate in state-mandated religious festivals. The Roman ruling class had little credence in their crowded pantheon and understood imperial divinity as purely political posture. Religious observance was a civic requirement, an individual's acknowledgment of the state's authority. The political nature of ancient persecution is often overlooked. One rightly remembers the early martyrs as spiritual figures. Modern martyrs deserve to be commemorated for the religious beliefs they died for, not the fraudulent political charges by which the state prosecuted them.

Martyrs may resist secular authority, but the form of their dissent remains quintessentially Christian. They do not fight power by political means but by insisting that their conscience stands outside secular jurisdiction. Their resistance echoes Christ's answer to Pilate at His arraignment, "My kingdom is not of this world: if my kingdom were of this world, then would my servants fight." Christ's passion and death remains the model. As Woodward observes, the martyr repeats the pattern of Christ's sacrifice:

> The classic Christian martyr is an innocent victim who dies for the faith at the hand of a tyrant who is opposed to the faith. Like Jesus, the classical martyr does not seek death but freely accepts it when challenged to renounce his faith or otherwise act contrary to Christian values. Also like Jesus, the classical martyr forgives his or her enemies.

The martyr is neither a rebel nor a victim. The task is not armed resistance; nor is passive suffering the martyr's object. Persecution, agony, and death are only the by-products of the martyr's true vocation—to witness the truth uncompromised. The etymological root of *martyr* contains no hint of death or suffering. *Martyr* simply means "witness." The martyr lives by Christ's words to Pilate, "For this cause came I into the world, that I should bear witness to the truth." As W. H. Auden wrote, "In the special case of Christ, the God-Man dies to redeem sinful mankind; the ordinary human martyr dies to bear witness to what he believes to be a saving truth, to be shared by all men."

Imitatio Christi, the imitation of Christ, has been the guiding principle of believers since apostolic times. Each time and place requires Christians to emulate Jesus in different ways. The early propagation of Christianity demanded martyrdom. All the apostles but John died violently. The first converts understood Bonhoeffer's "cost of discipleship." Many brought a calm acceptance of the mortal danger of their faith. "For me to live is Christ," wrote Paul to the Philippians, "and to die is gain." The early martyrs understood, as Martin Luther observed in the Augsburg Confession, that the Church itself was the community of those "who are persecuted and martyred for the Gospel's sake." "The blood of the martyrs is seed," declared Tertullian. The tragic seasons of history determine when new seed must be sown.

The twentieth century has reminded all conscientious Christians of the full cost of discipleship, as millions followed Christ's example even unto death. "When Christ calls a man," wrote Bonhoeffer, "he bid him come and die." He continues:

> It may be a death like that of the first disciples who had to leave home and work to follow him, or it may be a death like Luther's, who had to leave the monastery and go out into the world. But it is the same death every time—death in Jesus Christ, the death of the old man at his call.

Roman commentators puzzled at the odd joy with which the early martyrs faced their executions. When the governor of Pergamum condemned Carpus and Papylus to death by agonizing torture, the two condemned men ran to the amphitheater to meet their fate more quickly. Their joy was the exhilaration of victory—not secular but spiritual triumph. It was the conviction that death would not only gain them personal salvation but also undermine the system that oppressed them. The near absurdity of this conviction in political terms needs no elaboration. Yet history repeatedly vindicates the martyr's wild idealism. Nazi Germany and the Soviet Union now belong to the past no less than imperial Rome. A tyrant can kill bodies but not ideas, especially not ideas the just consider worth dying for. The moral example of martyrs not only outlived the empires that persecuted them; it gradually transformed them.

Modern martyrs have understood the communal significance of their deaths. The examples of Christ and the early martyrs have shown them the efficacy of sacrifice. Two weeks before he was gunned down at the altar, Bishop Oscar Romero described his probable fate to a Mexican journalist. His words recall Paul and Tertullian as much as liberation theology:

> I have often been threatened with death. Nevertheless, as a Christian, I do not believe in death without resurrection. If they kill me, I shall arise in the Salvadoran people . . .

Martyrdom is a grace of God that I do not believe I deserve. But if God accepts the sacrifice of my life, let my blood be a seed of freedom . . . A bishop will die, but the church of God, which is the people, will never perish.

Likewise, in Tegel prison a few months before his death, Bonhoeffer jotted down, "Death is the supreme festival on the road to freedom." The martyr suffers joyfully because, as Bonhoeffer noted elsewhere, "suffering is the badge of true discipleship."

The martyr dies not only to preserve individual integrity but also to demonstrate the integrity of the entire Church. Each martyrdom implicitly strengthens the Communion of Saints, the spiritual interdependence of all Christians living and dead. If the role of martyrs is to face persecution and death, the duty of the living is to remember them. Remembrance of their sacrifice is the Church's consciousness of its own identity. Such commemoration has moral and political significance. "The struggle against power," wrote Milan Kundera, "is the struggle of memory against forgetting." To forget past persecution makes it easier for atrocities to be repeated. Planning the dismemberment of Poland and extermination of its population, Hitler dismissed suggestions that the world community would object to Germany's aggression with a chilling remark, "Who remembers the Armenians?"

No previous age mounted so vast or sustained an attack on Christianity as the twentieth century. International communism alone assaulted the church on a hitherto impossible scale. Yet by the end of the century communism has mostly passed away while the church survives. In fact, the combined persecutions of modern totalitarian states had at least one unintended but beneficial effect — Christian ecumenism.

The savage intolerance of modern totalitarian governments helped Christians of all persuasions to understand the essential unity of their beliefs. Their persecution has also enlarged Christian sympathy for Judaism, just as the Nazi Holocaust demonstrated the intrinsic evil of anti-Semitism. New wounds helped heal the lingering ones of the Reformation. Today Catholic, Orthodox, and Protestant are more likely to celebrate what unites them than the few things that keep them apart. Catholic bishops have developed an ecumenical martyrology. The Lutherans have added Pope John XXIII to their calendar of saints. Leaders of the Catholic, Orthodox, and Anglican branches of Christianity pray together publicly and concelebrate the sacraments. Even the book you now hold in your hands—written by members of diverse creeds—represents the fruit of modern persecution: the conviction that the church Christ instituted through his apostles should be one.

The totalitarian state will never comprehend the true power of the church. "The Pope!" scoffed Stalin. "How many divisions has he got?" Peter and Paul commanded no legions, and yet their deaths defeated an empire. For all their political expertise, Caesars, ancient and modern, have misjudged what they sought to abolish. "The power of the Church," wrote Pope John Paul II in *Crossing the Threshold of Hope*, "has lain in the witness of the saints, of those who made Christ's truth their own truth . . . in the Eastern and Western Churches these saints have never been lacking." John Paul continues:

> The saints of our century have been in large part martyrs. The totalitarian regimes which dominated Europe in the middle of the twentieth century added to their numbers. Concentration camps, death camps—which produced, among other things, the monstrous Holocaust of the Jews—revealed authentic saints among Catholics and Orthodox, and among Protestants as well . . . In eastern Europe the army of holy martyrs, especially among the Orthodox, is enormous . . . This is the great multitude of those who, as is said in the Book of Revelation, "follow the Lamb" (Rev. 14:4). They have completed in their death as martyrs the redemptive sufferings of Christ (Col. 1:24) and, at the same time, they have become the foundation of a new world, a new Europe, and a new civilization.

As Christianity enters its third millennium, the link between contemporary faith and its apostolic origins has been renewed. Like Christianity's initial century, our age has been invigorated by "a cloud of witnesses." The suffering of modern martyrs has been inconceivable, their loss in human terms immense. The challenge of contemporary Christianity is to resist the comfort of forgetting and allow their example to animate the church. "The blood of martyrs is the seed" only if the living cultivate the fruit of such sacrifice. These witnesses found the grace to offer their lives for an ideal. We pray for the grace to lead peaceful lives of equal integrity. Without facing a firing squad, we hope to share their prayer, *Omnia ad maiorem Dei gloriam.*

This Is What We Suffer: A Note on the Paintings of George Tooker

In 1950 when Abstract Expression was all the rage and representational art was declared hopelessly passé, a young painter in Greenwich Village began creating a series of haunting masterpieces in a realistic style. The paintings depicted ordinary people in everyday settings—offices, waiting rooms, subways, cafeterias—but conveyed in a manner that made the scenes seem fantastic, even supernatural. Today these dream-like paintings would be called Magical Realism, but that term did not yet exist in English. The artist was George Tooker.

Tooker's work survived and eventually flourished because he had a genius for creating images of modern life that seem simultaneously astonishing and ordinary. In *Lunch* (1964), rows of office workers hunch over their meals seemingly oblivious of one another. In *Teller* (1967), identical bank clerks sit listless isolated behind steel-barred counters. In *Subway* (1950), commuters stand, anxious and afraid, in a concrete underworld. Once seen, the paintings stay fixed in the memory.

Recognition came slowly. For many years Tooker existed on the margins of the art world. The artist was sixty-five when the first full-length book on his work appeared. He was eighty-seven when he received the National Medal of the Arts. Tooker never complained about neglect. He was too absorbed by his own contrarian passions. They led him to surprising places. When other young painters followed Pablo Picasso and Jackson Pollock, Tooker studied the early Renaissance master Piero della Francesca. When the leading critics praised abstract formalism, Tooker emphasized content. His central concern was never style. It was the human condition.

Even Tooker's creative process differed from the methods of his more celebrated contemporaries. The Abstract Expressionists practiced "action painting" in which paint was dripped, splashed, smeared, or even fingered onto the canvas in a self-consciously spontaneous performance. Tooker meticulously planned his paintings with preliminary drawings, arranging his figures in geometric perspective as carefully as an Old Master. Tooker even mixed his own paints using egg yolks and pigments—just as Giotto or Botticelli did before the introduction of oils. Tooker's mature paintings were executed in tempera, a difficult and unforgiving medium. He applied the tempera in tiny strokes, carefully layering the colors, taking weeks or months to finish a work.

Tooker not only shared technique with the Old Masters. He also adopted their metaphysical vision of painting which tries simultaneously to present both the body and the soul of a subject. Tooker's artistic development reflects the slow transformation of his spirit. His early work emanated existential anxiety and terror. The intervening years were marked by his struggle for identity and meaning. His later work presents mysterious states of rapture, vision, and grace. Shortly after the death of Tooker's partner, William Christopher, in 1973, the artist resettled permanently in Vermont. Three years later he joined the Catholic Church.

Tooker's Catholicism was both genuine and profound. His partner's death provided the catalyst, but the artist's conversion reflected his lifelong search for community, justice, and religious faith. For years, he had followed Dorothy Day's *Catholic Worker* and participated in the Civil Rights Movement. His early paintings contained subtle Christian themes and symbols, which simply became more explicit after his conversion. At his parish church St. Francis of Assisi in Windsor, Vermont, Tooker attended daily Mass and helped distribute the Eucharist. He patterned his daily life on Franciscan simplicity.

When the church was destroyed by fire, the pastor asked Tooker to contribute a painting for a charity auction. Instead, the artist offered to create a new altarpiece when the church was rebuilt. In 1980 he finished *The Seven Sacraments*, a powerful recreation of the Renaissance tradition. Each of the seven panels presents a sacrament in contemporary terms. The kneeling penitent in the radiant and compassionate depiction of "Reconciliation" is Tooker's self-portrait. Four years later he painted the fourteen Stations of the Cross. No American Catholic church has more impressive paintings than this modest parish.

Tooker's originality is understated but abundant, though he never calls attention to his own innovation. What is most new in his paintings is inextricable from what is most ancient, because the two impulses have merged into the same vision. Let one example of his visionary originality suggest his meaningful newness. Starting in the late 1940s, Tooker began mingling the races in his work—white, black, Latin, mixed. The inclusivity is striking. The gesture has resonance, but race itself is never the real subject. His paintings depict the trials and redemption of all humanity. "In one kind of painting," he disclosed, "I'm trying to say 'this is what we are forced to suffer,' while in other paintings I say, 'this is what we should be.'"

George Tooker never met the critical expectations of the art world. He was both too far behind the times and too far ahead of them. But history has vindicated his outsider's vision of the spiritual struggles and consolations of the modern age. When he died in 2011 at the age of ninety, the *New York Times* praised him as "one of the most distinctive and mysterious painters of the twentieth century." By then the press was only stating the obvious.

The Cosmopolitan and the Campesino: The Sacred Sculpture of Luis Tapia

There is so much activity and variety in the American visual arts that it is difficult to assess the significance of any individual artist, especially one still productive and unpredictable. Over the last quarter century, however, it has become clear that the sculptor Luis Tapia has accomplished something singular, important, and slightly surprising. He has reconceptualized one of the oldest traditions of Latino and American regional art—the *santero*'s craft devotional sculpture—in a way that is both strikingly original and deeply respectful of its origins. In the process, Tapia has not only redeemed this powerful but narrow tradition from the weight of its own past; he has given his personal revision of it an international presence, thereby elevating the distinctively Hispanic form of sculpture beyond its folkloric identity. Without losing his personal connection with the past, Tapia has transformed the restrictive roles of the *santero* and the *santo* into something meaningfully new—more fluent, contemporary, and expansive.

The art world is more accustomed to disruption and transgression than to transformative renewal. (What is more normative in art nowadays than transgression?) It is easier to renounce or mock the past than to master and reshape it to new ends. Assimilating the past, however, allows new work to carry powerful formal and cultural resonance, such as Tapia's adaptations of New Mexican Catholic folk subjects and symbolism into new secular and social contexts. Tapia does not approach the past with the distanced irony and intellectual condescension of artists such as John Currin or Jeff Koons. Tapia remains invested in the forms, themes, and techniques of the New Mexican Latino Catholic tradition. There is irony in his depiction of contemporary economic and racial relations between Anglos and

Latinos, rich and poor, but his attitude toward his subject matter is never detached.

The vibrancy of Tapia's ironic and incisive satire seems closer to Goya or Daumier than to his voguish urban contemporaries. If he is ironic, he is also big-hearted and vulnerably human. Tapia gains a particular kind of energy and authenticity in allowing the viewer to feel quite directly his complex and sometimes contradictory emotions. He is angry, amused, affectionate, rude, and reverent—often at the same time. Tapia is a visionary realist who visibly occupies the same daily world as the viewer but also discovers its hidden moral, indeed religious, resonances. He has made the devotional forms of the *santero* profane and political without diminishing their sacred authority.

Never distancing himself from his origins, Tapia has become a significant American artist of unique identity, personal style, and political power. He did not abandon his tradition; he transformed it. Tapia has emerged from the Latino, Catholic, Southwestern, rural, poor—five varieties of marginalization, all alien to the metropolitan world of contemporary American art. He has made each of those "minor" and patronized categories mean something different from his precursors. He has enlarged his tradition to make it capacious enough to contain his imagination and the complexities of contemporary Latino experience.

To discuss Tapia's artistic identity in cultural and sociological terms is clarifying, but it also risks losing the main reason he is worth discussing in the first place—his excellence and originality. Contemporary art labors under heavy clouds of ideological weather. Latino artists in particular are rarely allowed to exist as individuals; they are abstracted into representations of group consciousness. Tapia's art doesn't matter because it is Latino, culturally marginal, or politically engaged. His art matters because it is so powerfully expressive, memorable, and original on its own individual terms. Studied in depth, his oeuvre reveals itself to be intellectually ambitious, thematically diverse, stylistically inventive, and masterful in technique.

Tapia's particular genius is also refreshingly democratic and inclusive. His sculptures arrest the viewer's attention whether that person is culturally sophisticated or not. He has developed a visual language, drawn from both the Hispanic vernacular and elite traditions, that engages equally the cosmopolitan and the *campesino*. Significantly, his mostly small works hold the viewer's gaze in ways that are simultaneously pleasurable and painful.

Tapia is a conceptual artist. There are always ideas animating both his forms and subjects, but those concepts are not imposed on the works. The meanings emanate from the physical objects themselves. We enter his disturbing and darkly beautiful work not intellectually but intuitively through its iconic images and visual narratives. There is also a conspicuously joyful mastery in his sculptures. They remind us that art, even tragic art, works most potently through pleasure.

I worry that I have taken too many theoretical flights in describing Tapia's very sensuous and grounded art. If that has been the case, I blame him. I can't look at Tapia's work without it triggering complicated ideas and emotions. Whenever I see his work, I have the same unnerving experience. Is it because I'm Catholic? Or part Mexican? Because I grew up among immigrants and the working poor? My background surely affects my responses. I so rarely see those subjects and people handled with such dignity, humor, and originality. But mostly I blame Tapia's merciless imagination. Someone needs to tell him that his work requires a trigger warning.

Singing Aquinas in L.A.

When I was a child in parochial school, we began each morning with daily Mass. My mother worked nights, and no one in my family was an early riser. I inevitably arrived late to church. The nuns stared as I slipped in among my more punctual classmates in our assigned pews. This daily dose of shame was good training for later life. It made me immune to peer pressure.

The Mass, which was conducted entirely in Latin, meant little to me. I endured it respectfully as a mandatory exercise. I was relieved when the service ended and we filed off to our classrooms across the street. What impressed me was the church itself. St. Joseph's was larger than the old Los Angeles cathedral. It was one of only two buildings in my hometown of Hawthorne, California, that might have been called beautiful. (The other was the Plaza, an old movie palace—now torn down.) I liked being inside St. Joseph's lofty, cool interior, which was illuminated by tall stained-glass windows depicting the saints and apostles.

On the first Friday of each month, however, there was another ceremony called the Benediction. Having already attended Mass in the morning, we were marched into church again in the afternoon to participate in a short but elaborate ritual in honor of the Eucharist.

The priest, wearing a special mantle over his robes, entered accompanied by several altar boys. Candles were lit, and great suffocating clouds of incense dispersed. As the priest approached the altar, we sang a Latin hymn called *O Salutaris Hostia*. We read the verses from little laminated cards. I didn't know what the words meant. (I assumed *hostia* meant the communion host, which, of course, it didn't.) I liked singing the hymn, but it wasn't my favorite.

American Catholics have a different sense of sacred music from Protestants. Singing is less central to our traditions of worship. The gap was especially wide before the Second Vatican Council. Catholics then rarely sang in church. There was no music at ordinary Mass, even on Sundays. Music was reserved for high Mass on special feast days, and then the singing was mostly Latin chant. In my Los Angeles parish, 1960 didn't sound much different from 1660.

At Benediction, however, hymns played a central role. The music endowed the service with a sense of special occasion. Hearing St. Joseph's mighty organ fill the capacious church gave me a physical thrill. It was the most powerful live music I had ever heard. Add to that titanic rumbling the voices of seven hundred parochial school kids singing in Latin, led by a dozen Sisters of Providence, and you will divine my wonderment and awe.

As the priest opened the shining tabernacle at the center of the marble altar and placed the consecrated host in a golden monstrance, we stood to sing a short hymn in veneration of the Eucharist. This hymn, the *Tantum Ergo*, has haunted me for the past sixty years. At each service I waited for it to begin, then sang in a blissful trance. It always ended too soon.

Here is the hymn. If you don't know what the words mean, don't worry; neither did I. Nor do I intend to translate them now. That is the point of the essay.

> Tantum ergo Sacramentum
> Veneremur cernui:
> Et antiquum documentum
> Novo cedat ritui:
> Praestet fides supplementum
> Sensuum defectui.
>
> Genitori, Genitoque
> Laus et jubilatio,
> Salus, honor, virtus quoque
> Sit et benedictio:
> Procedenti ab utroque
> Compar sit laudatio.

By third grade, I had the text indelibly memorized, though the only word I understood was *sacramentum*. The literal meaning of the words seemed unimportant compared to the experience of singing. Back then I felt no genuine attachment to what the sisters reverently referred to as "the Blessed Sacrament." (That devotion came much later.) The Eucharist was mostly an abstract idea. I sensed a sanctity in which I could not participate. But as I stood singing this short hymn with all my friends and teachers, I physically felt enraptured and exhilarated in the act of veneration.

As an adult, I can't accurately judge whether that experience was spiritual or aesthetic. I suspect that those two categories of perception are more interdependent than most people believe, especially in a child. I do know from my earliest memories that *Tantum Ergo* struck me as penetratingly sublime. Those two minutes of each month were more beautiful than anything outside the church doors on the ugly streets of my hometown. The hymn acquired private meaning—a web of deep longings and associations, of intellectual and spiritual awakenings that I didn't yet understand.

I rarely received Communion, usually just at Christmas and Easter. We had been instructed only to receive the sacrament in "the state of grace." In my convoluted young mind, I was a notorious sinner. Even before puberty, I always felt guilty about something.

Being different from other kids—dreamy, solitary, bookish—my mere existence felt vaguely culpable. Unless I dashed directly from the confessional to the communion rail, I would stumble back into perdition. So it wasn't the Mass, which I attended listlessly six times a week, that brought me into the mysteries of faith; it was the infrequent Benedictions. Only there I momentarily lost my self-consciousness in joyful musical communion—singing ancient and enigmatic words in honor of an inexplicable transubstantiation.

In college I discovered that the intricately rhymed verses had been written by St. Thomas Aquinas for the new Feast of Corpus Christi the year before Dante was born. The poem, therefore, dates to a specific moment in Western culture. It appeared just as Latin was about to give way to Italian as a literary language, and the Middle Ages were moving toward the Renaissance. That fact now seems significant to me.

Babel was my hometown. I was raised in thirteenth-century L.A. in a Spanish-speaking neighborhood by Italian immigrants and as-similated mestizos who worshipped in Latin in a city whose official language was English. Latin was not a dead language; it was simply the one reserved for sacred things—like singing—in a place full of competing dialects. Even as a child, I watched my family's parlance change, as English superseded the languages of the older generation. No, the *Tantum Ergo* didn't feel foreign. Old words brought over from an old world were my daily reality.

The old practices, as Aquinas noted, give way to new rites (*Et antiquum documentum, / Novo cedat ritui*). By the time I finished high school, Vatican II had dropped Latin from the Mass and most rituals. We still prayed in Latin, but now only in Latin class when we stood to recite a quick *Pater Noster* before digging into another forty lines of Virgil. At Mass we now sang folksy anthems composed by amateur Jesuit musicians. If hell has a hymnal, these tunes will fill its opening pages. Hardly anyone sang. The crowd at Sunday Mass grew smaller every year.

No one recognized the banality of the new liturgy as keenly as a California teenager. For me, *aggiornamento* became *addio*. After graduating from high school in 1969, I stopped going to Mass for nearly twenty years, except on Christmas and Easter with my mother. I never left the Church. I just stopped showing up. The hunger remained, unsatisfied. Finally, in middle age, I accepted the bad music as punishment for my sins and rejoined as a communicant.

Over the years I have learned that I was not the only kid deeply affec-ted by the hymn. When the *Tantum Ergo* is mentioned to Catholics of my generation, often as not, somebody starts singing. I have watched that happen, even in bars. The words and tune arouse deep communal memories.

Aquinas's hymn even ended up in my libretto for the opera *Tony Caruso's Final Broadcast*. When I suggested employing the *Tantum Ergo* to the composer Paul Salerni, he immediately began singing the words over the phone. We ended up using the melody twice in the opera—once with the traditional words and tune, then later with the melody inverted to create a new chorale. A few years later, over lunch at the USC faculty club, I mentioned the hymn to the historian Kevin Starr. After singing the first stanza, he provided a theological exposition in his booming voice. "'*Praestet fides supplementum*,' Dana! 'Faith provides a supplement for the defects of our senses!'" Conversation stopped at nearby tables. Yes, the hymn has an alarming effect on old Catholics.

My particular affection for the hymn probably originates in a combination of personal and impersonal factors. First, there was the resonant beauty of Aquinas's verse set to the stately eighteenth-century tune by Samuel Webbe. Second, there was my personal experience of singing the words repeatedly for years with my friends in the first grand space I had ever seen. Finally, there was the mystery of the Eucharist, which I first understood not from theological instruction but through the beauty of song.

As an artist, I learned something else from the Latin hymns—that art is mysterious. It reaches us in ways we don't fully understand. The literal sense of a song or a poem is only part of its meaning. Physical sound and rhythm exercise a power of enchantment that eludes paraphrase. Our intuition often outpaces our intellect, and music anticipates meaning. He who sings prays twice, sometimes unaware.

Dana Gioia is the Poet Laureate of California. He is the author of five collections of verse, including *Interrogations at Noon* (2001), which won the American Book Award, and *99 Poems: New & Selected* (2016), which won the Poets' Prize. His critical collections include *Can Poetry Matter?* (1992), which was a finalist for the National Book Critics Award. He has written four opera libretti and edited over twenty literary anthologies. For six years Gioia served as Chairman of the National Endowment for the Arts where he helped create the largest programs in the agency's history and was recognized as "the man who saved the NEA." He has received the Laetare Medal from Notre Dame, Presidential Citizens Medal, and Aiken-Taylor Award in Modern Poetry. Gioia holds the Judge Widney Chair of Poetry and Public Culture at the University of Southern California.